From our Kitchen to Yours

ALL-TIME-FAVORITE RECIPES

From

INDIANA

COOKS

T0061940

Dedication

For every cook who wants to create amazing
recipes from the great state of Indiana.

Appreciation

Thanks to all our Indiana cooks who shared their
delightful and delicious recipes with us!

Gooseberry Patch
An imprint of Globe Pequot
64 South Main Street
Essex, CT 06426
www.gooseberrypatch.com
1 800 854 6673

Copyright 2022, Gooseberry Patch
978-1-6209-3506-4

Do you have a tried & true recipe...tip, craft or
memory that you'd like to see featured in a
Gooseberry Patch cookbook? Visit our website at
www.gooseberrypatch.com and follow the easy steps
to submit your favorite family recipe.

Or send them to us at:

    Gooseberry Patch
    PO Box 812
    Columbus, OH 43216-0812

Don't forget to include the number of servings your
recipe makes, plus your name, address, phone
number and email address. If we select your recipe,
your name will appear right along with it... and you'll
receive a FREE copy of the book!

INDIANA COOKS

ICONIC INDIANA

While Indiana's culture was influenced by France and Great Britain as well as German and Irish immigrants, it is no surprise that because of its earliest history with Native American culture, Indiana was dubbed the name "Indiana." Because of its Native American heritage, today, Indiana is the leader in production of one of America's most fancied foods - corn (and popcorn)!

Throughout its history, each heritage planted its traditions and cultural ways into the Hoosier state, creating a diverse mixture of practices and traditions that influence many of the cuisines enjoyed by Indiana residents today.

Although many Hoosiers may want to challenge on the basketball court, the speedway track or the football field, there is no denying that Indiana has produced some of the finest cooks around and with their diversely delectable cuisines, everything on the menu is a sure win!

Inside this collection you'll find delicious tried & true recipes from cooks from all around the great state of Indiana, including Pork Tenderloin Sandwich, Whipping Cream Waffles & Cranberry Butter, Ranch Cornbread Salad, Big Game Sloppy Joes, Pub Beer Dip, Raspberry Custard Pie and more!

From the top of the highest sand dune to the vast, open farmlands, it is clear that the Hoosiers really know their way around the kitchen and have shared recipes that are spirited and dear to their hearts. Enjoy!

OUR STORY

Back in 1984, our families were neighbors in little Delaware, Ohio. With small children, we wanted to do what we loved and stay home with the kids too. We had always shared a love of home cooking and so, **Gooseberry Patch** was born.

Almost immediately, we found a connection with our customers and it wasn't long before these friends started sharing recipes. Since then we've enjoyed publishing hundreds of cookbooks with your tried & true recipes.

We know we couldn't have done it without our friends all across the country and we look forward to continuing to build a community with you. Welcome to the **Gooseberry Patch** family!

JoAnn & Vickie

TABLE OF CONTENTS

CHAPTER ONE

BIG FOUR BRIDGE

Breakfasts

ENJOY THESE TASTY BREAKFAST RECIPES THAT BRING YOU TO THE TABLE WITH A HEARTY "GOOD MORNING!" AND CARRY YOU THROUGH THE DAY TO TACKLE WHATEVER COMES YOUR WAY.

BUSY-MORNING BANANA BREAD

LAURA JUSTICE
INDIANAPOLIS, IN

Super easy and freezes well. Just pull from the freezer the night before and it will be ready for your busy morning!

3 ripe bananas, mashed
3 eggs, beaten
1/2 c. butter, melted and slightly cooled
1 T. vanilla extract
1/2 c. water
18-1/2 oz. pkg. yellow cake mix

In a large bowl, blend together bananas, eggs, butter, vanilla and water. Gradually add dry cake mix. Beat with an electric mixer on high speed for 4 minutes. Pour batter into 2 greased 9"x5" loaf pans. Bake at 350 degrees for 40 minutes. Increase temperature to 400 degrees and bake an additional 5 to 10 minutes, until tops are golden.

Makes 2 loaves.

KITCHEN TIP

A crock of honey butter...so yummy on warm bread, biscuits and muffins. Simply blend together 1/2 cup each of honey and softened butter.

SOUTHERN VEGGIE BRUNCH CASSEROLE

JENNIFER MCCLURE
LEBANON, IN

Our family always has this breakfast dish for dinner, and it's fondly called "brinner" by our two children.

In a greased 3-quart casserole dish, layer sausage, onions, peppers, tomatoes and cheese. In a large bowl, whisk together remaining ingredients; pour over cheese. Bake, uncovered, at 350 degrees for 55 to 60 minutes, until set and top is golden. Let stand for 10 minutes before serving.

Serves 6 to 8.

1 lb. ground pork sausage, browned and drained

1/2 c. green onions, chopped

1 green pepper, diced

1 red pepper, diced

1 jalapeño pepper, seeded and diced

2 tomatoes, chopped

2 c. shredded mozzarella cheese

1 c. biscuit baking mix

1 doz. eggs, beaten

1 c. milk

1/2 t. dried oregano

1/2 t. salt

1/4 t. pepper

PUMPKIN PANCAKES

CRIS GOODE
MOORESVILLE, IN

When I make these pancakes with my daughter, we use cookie cutters to cut them into fun shapes! Serve with butter and syrup, or try cream cheese or pumpkin dip for a special treat.

2 c. biscuit baking mix
1/2 c. canned pumpkin
1 c. water
1 egg white, beaten
2 t. pumpkin pie spice
Garnish: butter,
  pancake syrup

Combine all ingredients except garnish in a bowl; beat well. Pour batter onto a greased griddle by 1/4 cupfuls. Cook over medium heat until golden on both sides. Serve with butter and syrup.

Makes 6 servings.

CORNMEAL MUSH

PAM HOOLEY
LAGRANGE, IN

This is a favorite from our childhoods. My husband loves it with gravy,
and I love it with maple syrup, very cheap and filling.

Bring 3 cups water to a boil in a saucepan over medium heat. In a bowl, mix remaining water with cornmeal, flour and salt. Whisk into boiling water and stir until thickened. Cover and simmer over low heat for 20 minutes, stirring occasionally. Pour cornmeal mixture into a lightly greased 9"x5" loaf pan. Cover and refrigerate until set. To serve, turn out of pan; cut into thin slices. Roll slices in flour; cook in butter in a skillet over medium-high heat until golden on both sides.

Serves 2 to 3.

4 c. cold water, divided
1 c. cornmeal
1/4 c. all-purpose flour
1 t. salt
additional flour as
  needed
butter for frying

PEANUT BUTTER FRENCH TOAST

JULIE ANN PERKINS
ANDERSON, IN

Who can resist the classic taste of peanut butter & jelly?

4 slices white or whole-wheat bread

1/2 c. creamy peanut butter

2 T. grape jelly

3 eggs, beaten

1/4 c. milk

2 T. butter

Garnish: powdered sugar

Use bread, peanut butter and jelly to make 2 sandwiches; set aside. In a bowl, whisk together eggs and milk. Dip each sandwich into egg mixture. Melt butter in a non-stick skillet over medium heat. Add sandwiches to skillet and cook until golden, about 2 to 3 minutes on each side. Sprinkle with powdered sugar; cut diagonally into triangles.

Makes 2.

JUST FOR FUN

Paleo-Indians are said to be the first inhabitants of Indiana. By the end of the Ice Age, when the glaciers melted, they arrived around 8000 BCE. They were nomads and could hunt large creatures like mastodons.

KRISTA'S BREAKFAST TACOS

KRISTA MARSHALL
FORT WAYNE, IN

I created these fun and tasty tacos for breakfast or brunch when I discovered taco-size tortillas are easier for my son Alex to handle than the large burrito-size ones.

In a large skillet over medium heat, brown sausage until no longer pink. Drain sausage and remove to a bowl, reserving one tablespoon drippings; set aside. In same skillet, sauté green pepper and half of tomatoes in reserved drippings until tender. In a large bowl, whisk eggs, cream, 1/3 cup cheese, salt and pepper. When pepper mixture is tender, reduce heat to low; add egg mixture and sausage. Cook over low heat, stirring constantly, until eggs are scrambled and cooked through, about 10 minutes. Fill tortillas with egg mixture. Top with remaining tomatoes, cheese and avocado, if desired.

Makes 8 tacos.

1 lb. mild or hot ground pork breakfast sausage

1 green pepper, finely chopped

3 to 4 tomatoes, chopped and divided

8 eggs, beaten

2 T. whipping cream

1 c. shredded taco-blend cheese, divided

salt and pepper to taste

8 taco-size flour tortillas

Optional: sliced avocado

HONEY CRUNCH GRANOLA

**EMILY HARTZELL
PORTLAND, IN**

For a delicious, healthy breakfast, serve over vanilla yogurt with fresh berries and bananas!

4 c. long-cooking oats, uncooked

1/2 c. unsalted slivered almonds

1/4 c. unsalted sunflower kernels

1/2 c. honey

1/2 c. butter

2 t. cinnamon

1/8 t. ground cloves

1 t. vanilla extract

1/8 t. salt

Mix oats, almonds and sunflower kernels in a large bowl; set aside. Combine honey, butter, spices, vanilla and salt in a microwave-safe bowl. Microwave on high setting until butter and honey are melted; stir well. Pour honey mixture over oat mixture; toss until well coated. Spread on a lightly greased 15"x10" jelly-roll pan. Bake at 350 degrees for 20 minutes, or until lightly golden. Allow to cool completely; store in an airtight container.

Makes 8 servings.

STEAK & EGG HASH

LILY JAMES
FORT WAYNE, IN

This is a hearty breakfast my family really loves.

Heat oil in a skillet over medium heat. Add beef cubes; sprinkle with seasonings. Cook beef cubes until no longer pink. Remove beef to a plate, reserving drippings in skillet. Add potatoes to skillet; cook until golden, stirring occasionally. Add onion; cook until soft and potatoes are cooked through. Return beef to skillet; reduce heat to low. With the back of a spoon, make 3 to 6 shallow wells in potato mixture; gently crack an egg into each well. Sprinkle with tomatoes. Cover and cook until eggs reach desired doneness.

Makes 3 to 6 servings.

1 to 2 T. olive oil
1-1/2 lbs. beef sirloin
   steak, cut into 1-inch
   cubes
1/4 t. salt
1/4 t. pepper
1/4 t. garlic powder
1 lb. potatoes, peeled and
   diced
1 onion, chopped
3 to 6 eggs
1 c. tomatoes, diced

APPLE CUSTARD COFFEE CAKE

KATHY GRASHOFF
FORT WAYNE, IN

I love when it's fall and the apples are plentiful! Try this delicious coffee cake recipe with pears too.

2 c. biscuit baking mix

1 c. sugar, divided

3/4 c. milk

1 t. vanilla extract

1 c. chopped pecans

2 tart apples, peeled, cored and chopped

1 t. cinnamon, divided

3 eggs, beaten

1 c. whipping cream

In a large bowl, combine baking mix, 1/4 cup sugar, milk and vanilla; mix well. Stir in pecans; pour batter into a greased 9"x9" baking pan and set aside. In a separate bowl, toss apples with 1/4 cup sugar and 1/2 teaspoon cinnamon; spoon apples over batter. In a bowl, combine eggs, cream and remaining sugar; pour over apples. Sprinkle with remaining cinnamon. Bake, uncovered, at 350 degrees for 40 to 45 minutes, until a knife tip inserted in the center comes out clean. Serve warm.

Makes 9 servings.

APPLE CIDER SYRUP

PAM HOOLEY
LAGRANGE, IN

*This is a delicious substitute for maple syrup whenever you're having
pancakes or waffles.*

In a small saucepan over medium heat, stir together
sugar or honey, cornstarch and cinnamon. Add apple
juice and lemon juice; bring to a boil. Cook and stir
for 2 minutes. Remove from heat; add butter and stir
until melted. Syrup will thicken as it cools.

Serves 4.

1/4 c. sugar or honey
4 t. cornstarch
1/2 t. cinnamon
1 c. apple cider or apple
   juice
1 T. lemon juice
2 T. butter

GOLDEN FRUIT COMPOTE

LAURA FULLER
FORT WAYNE, IN

This is a recipe Mom tried one Christmas after finding it in a magazine. It was a hit! Wonderful at brunch, or with baked ham or pork. The canned figs aren't so easy to find anymore, but you can substitute dried figs simmered in water until they're plump.

29-oz. can peach halves, drained

29-oz. can pear halves, drained

20-oz. can pineapple rings, drained

15-oz. can Kadota figs, drained

1/2 c. brown sugar, packed

1/3 c. butter

1 t. ground ginger

3/4 t. curry powder

1/8 t. salt

Combine all fruits in a 2-1/2 quart casserole dish; set aside. In a small saucepan, combine remaining ingredients. Bring to a boil over medium heat; cook and stir until brown sugar dissolves. Drizzle mixture over fruit; mix gently. Bake, uncovered, at 350 degrees for 40 minutes, basting occasionally with liquid in dish. Serve warm.

Makes 8 servings.

PRESENTATION

If you're planning a family gathering, decorate your table to bring back childhood memories. Glue photocopies of old family photos to heavy paper for personalized table centerpieces.

SAVORY CHEESE MUFFINS

KATHY GRASHOFF
FORT WAYNE, IN

Yummy with breakfast or alongside a bowl of soup! Make them even better by adding some crumbled bacon.

In a bowl, combine flour, baking powder, salt and pepper; set aside. Lightly beat egg in another bowl; stir in olive oil, milk and dill weed. Stir in cheese. Add egg mixture to flour mixture; stir with a fork until just combined. Divide batter evenly among 6 greased muffin cups. Bake at 450 degrees for about 8 to 10 minutes, until golden and a toothpick comes out clean. Serve warm.

Makes 6 muffins.

1 c. plus 2 T. all-purpose flour
2 t. baking powder
1/4 t. salt
1/8 t. pepper
1 egg
1/4 c. olive oil
1/2 c. milk
3/4 t. dried dill weed
1 c. shredded extra-sharp Cheddar cheese

GRANDMA'S EGGS CHEDDAR

CAROLYN DECKARD
BEDFORD, IN

Whenever we were lucky enough to stay overnight at Grandma's on Christmas Eve, on Christmas morning she would fix this wonderful breakfast for us. It's still special to me.

2 green onions, chopped

1 T. butter

10-3/4 oz. can tomato soup

16-oz. pkg. shredded sharp Cheddar cheese

1/2 t. dry mustard

1/4 t. dried basil

salt and pepper to taste

3 eggs, beaten

1-1/2 c. milk

4 slices French bread, cut 2 inches thick and lightly toasted

Garnish: chopped fresh parsley

In a skillet over medium heat, sauté onions in butter until golden. Reduce heat to low; add soup, cheese and seasonings. Cook and stir until well blended and cheese is melted. In a bowl, whisk together eggs and milk; add to cheese mixture. Cook until eggs are lightly set. Arrange toast in the bottom of a lightly greased 9"x9" baking pan. Spoon cheese mixture over toast. Bake, uncovered, at 350 degrees for 15 minutes, or until golden on top. Garnish with parsley.

Makes 4 servings.

GARDEN BOUNTY EGG BAKE

**LISA SANDERS
SHOALS, IN**

I came up with this easy recipe to help my husband Jim enjoy eating more vegetables. He loves eggs, so what better way to get him to eat veggies! Yummy served with biscuits and jelly. For an extra-hearty breakfast, add one cup cooked and crumbled bacon or sausage.

In a bowl, whisk together eggs and milk; stir in seasonings and set aside. Heat oil in a large ovenproof skillet over medium-high heat. Add all vegetables except tomato; sauté until crisp-tender. Add tomato to skillet. Pour egg mixture over vegetable mixture; remove skillet to the oven. Bake at 350 degrees for about 15 to 20 minutes, until a knife tip inserted in the center tests clean. Sprinkle with cheese; return to oven until cheese melts. Serve with hot pepper sauce, if desired.

Makes 6 servings.

1 doz. eggs
1/2 c. milk
1 T. dried parsley
1 t. dried thyme
1 t. garlic powder
salt and pepper to taste
1 T. olive oil
8-oz. pkg. sliced
  mushrooms
1/2 c. onion, diced
1/2 c. green pepper, diced
1/2 c. carrot, peeled and
  shredded
1/2 c. broccoli, chopped
1/2 c. tomato, chopped
1 c. shredded mild
  Cheddar cheese
Optional: hot pepper
  sauce

CHEESY EGG CASSEROLE

LYNN WILLIAMS
MUNCIE, IN

This is a treat-yourself kind of weekend breakfast. If it's going to be a busy morning, prep the egg and sausage mixtures ahead of time; refrigerate separately. In the morning, just combine in the pressure cooker and go!

1 c. shredded Cheddar cheese

8 eggs, beaten

1/2 c. milk

1 t. salt, divided

1/2 t. pepper, divided

1 t. olive oil

1/2 lb. pork breakfast sausages

1 c. yellow onion, chopped

1 c. red pepper, chopped

2 T. fresh chives, minced

1 c. water

Garnish: sour cream

Wrap a 7" springform pan with aluminum foil, leaving some excess for handles on each side. Spray pan with non-stick vegetable spray; spread cheese in pan and set aside. In a bowl, whisk together eggs, milk, 1/2 teaspoon salt and 1/4 teaspoon pepper. Set aside. Add oil to a 5-quart electric pressure cooker; set on sauté. Add sausages; cook, stirring often, until browned. Add onion and red pepper; cook, stirring often, until tender. Stir in chives and remaining salt and pepper; transfer sausage mixture to pan. Place a rack or trivet inside pressure cooker; add water. Set pan on rack; pour egg mixture over sausage mixture. Close and lock lid; cook on high pressure for 12 minutes. Open pressure cooker using natural release method; let stand 10 minutes. Using the foil handles, remove pan from pressure cooker. Cut into wedges; serve with sour cream.

Serves 6 to 8.

GOOEY CINNAMON ROLLS

LAURA FULLER
FORT WAYNE, IN

These go together in a jiffy! Then on Saturdays, when my sisters and I get back from early-morning garage sales, we enjoy these rolls together with some hot coffee.

Spray a 4-quart slow cooker with non-stick vegetable spray. Arrange half of cinnamon roll pieces in the bottom of slow cooker; set aside icing packets. In a small bowl, whisk together eggs, cream, maple syrup, vanilla and spices. Spoon over cinnamon rolls in slow cooker. Layer remaining cinnamon roll pieces on top; drizzle one packet of icing over rolls. Cover and cook on low setting for 2 to 2-1/2 hours, until rolls are set and golden at the sides. Remove crock from slow cooker. Drizzle remaining icing packet over top; sprinkle with nuts, if using. Serve warm.

Serves 6 to 8.

2 12-oz. tubes
  refrigerated cinnamon
  rolls, cut into quarters
  and divided
4 eggs, beaten
1/2 c. whipping cream
1/4 c. pure maple syrup
2 t. vanilla extract
1 t. cinnamon
1 t. nutmeg
Optional: 1/2 c. chopped
  pecans

FAMILY-TIME CONVERSATION

Indiana University and Purdue University wanted to stand out among the many institutions in the U.S., by signifying their rivalry and attracting attention. Both schools decided that they would take a bucket surrounded with numerous metallic I's and P's, to make it look like a trophy. It's called the "oaken bucket," and the two schools battle over it every year during football season.

WHIPPING CREAM WAFFLES & CRANBERRY BUTTER

KATHY GRASHOFF
FORT WAYNE, IN

I just love waffles on a snowy morning with nowhere to rush off to!

8-oz. container
  whipping cream
2 eggs, separated
1 T. butter, melted and
  slightly cooled
2/3 c. all-purpose flour
1/3 c. sugar
1 t. baking powder
1/8 t. salt

CRANBERRY BUTTER

1/2 c. butter, softened
1/4 c. powdered sugar
2 T. whole-berry
  cranberry sauce

In a deep bowl, beat cream with an electric mixer on medium speed until soft peaks form. In a separate bowl, beat egg yolks with a fork until thick and light-colored; fold in whipped cream and butter. Combine remaining ingredients, except egg whites, in a small bowl; fold into whipped cream mixture. Beat egg whites on high speed until stiff peaks form; fold into batter. Batter will be thick. For each waffle, spoon half of batter onto a preheated, oiled waffle iron, spreading to edges. Bake according to manufacturer's directions, until crisp and lightly golden. Serve with Cranberry Butter.

Cranberry Butter:

Combine butter and powdered sugar; beat with an electric mixer on medium speed until blended. Stir in cranberry sauce; chill.

Makes 2 servings.

SPICED HARVEST PANCAKES

SHELLY SMITH
DANA, IN

A wonderful waker-upper on a cool fall morning!

Stir together all ingredients until well blended. Pour about 1/4 cup of batter per pancake onto a hot griddle that has been sprayed with non-stick vegetable spray. Cook over medium heat until pancakes start to bubble; flip and cook until golden.

Makes about one dozen.

2-1/2 c. biscuit baking mix
1 c. milk
1 c. apple butter
2 T. oil
1/2 t. ground ginger
1/2 t. cinnamon
1/2 t. nutmeg
2 eggs, beaten

PECAN PIE MUFFINS

MELYNDA HOFFMAN
FORT WAYNE, IN

When my daughter Brooke took these scrumptious muffins to the Allen County Fair, she won a blue ribbon. All the judges asked for another muffin...please! We make them for our holiday breakfasts, but they're a great treat anytime.

1 c. chopped pecans
1 c. brown sugar, packed
1/2 c. all-purpose flour
2 eggs
1/2 c. butter or coconut oil, melted and cooled slightly

Mix pecans, brown sugar and flour in a large bowl; make a well in the center and set aside. In a separate bowl, beat eggs just until foam appears. Stir in butter or oil. Add pecan mixture; stir just until moistened. Spoon batter into muffin cups greased only on the bottom, filling about 2/3 full. Bake at 350 degrees for 20 to 25 minutes, until golden. Promptly remove from muffin tin; cool on a wire rack.

Makes 9.

JUST FOR FUN

According to an old law that's still on the books, in Indiana, mustaches are illegal if the bearer of the mustaches has an addiction to kissing people.

  Indiana

ALL-IN-ONE SUNRISE CASSEROLE

JESSICA ROBERTSON
FISHERS, IN

Equally delicious made with crisply cooked bacon or cubed baked ham instead of sausage. Add a simple fruit cup and breakfast is ready to go!

The night before, place a layer of hashbrowns in the bottom of a slow cooker, followed by a layer of sausage, then onion, green pepper and cheese. Repeat layering 2 to 3 more times, ending with cheese on top. Whisk together eggs, milk, salt and pepper; pour over layers in slow cooker. Cover and cook on low setting overnight for 7 to 8 hours.

Makes 6 to 8 servings.

32-oz. pkg. frozen shredded hashbrowns

1 lb. ground turkey breakfast sausage links or patties, browned and drained

1 onion, diced

1 green pepper, diced

1-1/2 c. shredded Cheddar cheese

1 doz. eggs, beaten

1 c. milk

1 t. salt

1 t. pepper

KITCHEN TIP

For hosting a stress-free brunch, focus on make-ahead meals like baked French toast and egg casseroles. Save recipes that need to be cooked on the spot, like pancakes and omelets, for smaller family breakfasts.

DARK CHOCOLATE CHIP PUMPKIN MUFFINS

SARA VOGES
WASHINGTON, IN

I love to share this recipe with family & friends...everyone needs a good healthy breakfast treat!

4 eggs, beaten
1 c. sugar
15-oz. can pumpkin
1 c. applesauce
1/2 c. oil
3 c. whole-wheat flour
2 t. baking powder
2 t. baking soda
1 t. salt
1 t. cinnamon
12-oz. pkg. dark chocolate chips

In a large bowl, combine eggs, sugar, pumpkin, applesauce and oil; beat until smooth. In another bowl, combine remaining ingredients except chocolate chips; mix well. Add flour mixture to egg mixture; stir well. Fold in chocolate chips. Spoon batter into 24 greased muffin cups, filling 3/4 full. Bake at 400 degrees for 16 to 20 minutes.

Makes 2 dozen.

GOLDENROD EGGS

LYNN WILLIAMS
MUNCIE, IN

My grandmother raised chickens on her small farm and sometimes she'd send me to collect the eggs. If I found enough eggs, she made this dish of creamed eggs on toast for us to share.

Remove yolks from eggs; place in a bowl and mash with a fork. Chop egg whites and place in another bowl; set both aside. Melt butter in a saucepan over medium-low heat. Stir in flour until smooth; cook and stir until bubbly. Gradually whisk in milk until smooth. Bring to a boil, stirring constantly. Add mashed egg yolks and bouillon; stir until thoroughly combined. Add chopped egg whites; mix well. Season with salt and pepper. To serve, spoon egg mixture over buttered toast; sprinkle with paprika.

Makes 4 servings.

8 eggs, hard-boiled, peeled and halved
1/4 c. butter
1/4 c. all-purpose flour
2 c. milk
2 t. chicken bouillon granules
salt and pepper to taste
4 slices bread, toasted and buttered
paprika to taste

HOMEMADE PANCAKE SYRUP

CAROLYN GOCHENAUR
HOWE, IN

*My friend Brenda shared this recipe with me. I made it many times
when my children were still living at home.*

1 c. sugar
1 c. water
1 c. brown sugar, packed
Optional: 3/4 t. maple
flavoring
1 c. light corn syrup

In a saucepan over medium heat, combine all ingredients except maple flavoring. Bring to a boil, stirring constantly. Remove from heat; stir in flavoring, if using. Syrup will thicken as it cools. May cover and refrigerate up to 2 weeks.

Makes 15 servings.

JUST FOR FUN

Indiana produces more popcorn than any other state. Orville Redenbacher himself was born in Brazil, Indiana, and there's even a town named Popcorn, Indiana!

CITRUS-GLAZED FRUIT SALAD

PAMELA MYERS
AUBURN, IN

This fruit salad is the absolute best! I can't tell you how many times I've been asked for the recipe. I serve it with sweet rolls for breakfast and with cake for dessert. The glaze prevents the fruit from turning brown, so it keeps well for a few days in the refrigerator. Change up the fruit to suit your family's taste...I've also used apples and kiwi.

In a serving bowl, combine all of the fruit; set aside. In a saucepan, combine reserved pineapple juice, orange juice, lemon juice, sugar and cornstarch. Cook and stir over medium heat until thickened and bubbly. Remove from heat; set aside. Pour warm sauce over fruit and stir gently to coat. Cover and refrigerate.

Makes 12 to 16 servings.

4 c. strawberries, hulled and sliced

4 c. blueberries

2 c. seedless green grapes, halved

2 to 3 ripe bananas, sliced

11-oz. can mandarin oranges, drained

20-oz. can pineapple tidbits, drained and juice reserved

1/3 c. orange juice

1 T. lemon juice

1/2 c. sugar

2 T. cornstarch

BERRY-PICKER'S REWARD MUFFINS

NANCY PORTER
FORT WAYNE, IN

This recipe works well with blueberries and strawberries too.

1/2 c. margarine, softened
1-1/4 c. sugar
2 eggs, beaten
8-oz. container sour cream
1 t. vanilla extract
2 c. all-purpose flour
1 t. baking powder
1/2 t. baking soda
1/4 t. salt
1 c. raspberries
3 T. margarine, melted

TOPPING
2 T. sugar
1/4 t. nutmeg
1/4 t. cinnamon

With an electric mixer on medium-high speed, beat softened margarine for 30 seconds. Add sugar; beat until combined. Blend in eggs, sour cream and vanilla. Use a spoon to stir in dry ingredients until just moistened; fold in berries. Spoon batter into paper-lined or greased muffin cups, filling 2/3 full. Bake at 400 degrees for 18 to 20 minutes, until a toothpick tests clean. Brush tops of hot muffins with melted margarine; sprinkle with topping. Cool in pan for 5 minutes; transfer to a wire rack to finish cooling.

Topping:

Combine all ingredients in a small bowl.

Makes 20.

LIGHT BLUEBERRY DANISH

MOLLY EBERT
COLUMBUS, IN

This is an old recipe I reworked to make it lower in fat. It's still delicious...just as good as the original!

Unroll dough into 4 rectangles; firmly press perforations together to seal. In a bowl, blend cheese and sugar; spread onto dough rectangles to within 1/2 inch of edges. Top evenly with blueberries. Bring opposite corners of rectangles together; press together to seal. Place on an ungreased baking sheet. Bake at 375 degrees for 15 to 18 minutes, until golden.

Makes 4 servings.

8-oz. tube refrigerated reduced- fat crescent dinner rolls

1/2 c. Neufchâtel or light cream cheese, softened

2 T. sugar or powdered sweetener

1/2 c. fresh blueberries

YUMMY BRUNCH STRATA

LYNN WILLIAMS
MUNCIE, IN

*My grandma was famous for this feed-a-crowd dish at the weekly
brunch her church used to hold after Sunday services. Just add a tray
of sweet rolls, a big pot of hot coffee and fellowship!*

1/3 c. oil
2 c. cooked ham, diced
3 c. sliced mushrooms
3 c. zucchini, diced
1-1/2 c. onion, diced
1-1/2 c. green, red or
  yellow pepper, diced
2 cloves garlic, minced
2 8-oz. pkgs. cream
  cheese, softened
1/2 c. half-and-half
1 doz. eggs, beaten
4 c. day-old bread, cubed
3 c. shredded Cheddar
  cheese
salt and pepper to taste

Heat oil in a large skillet over medium-high heat.
Add ham and vegetables; sauté for 3 to 5 minutes,
until tender. Drain; set aside. In a large bowl, beat
together cream cheese and half-and-half until
smooth. Stir in vegetable mixture and remaining
ingredients; blend lightly. Pour into 2 greased
11"x7" baking pans. Bake, uncovered, at 350
degrees for 35 to 40 minutes, until a knife inserted
near the center comes out clean. Let stand
10 minutes; cut into squares.

Makes 16 servings.

FRENCH TOAST CROISSANTS

KATHY GRASHOFF
FORT WAYNE, IN

When summer mornings beckon with so much to do, this breakfast is quick & easy!

Stir milk, eggs and orange juice together in a shallow dish. Dip croissant halves into mixture, turning to coat both sides. Place in a greased skillet over medium heat; cook until golden on both sides. Dust with powdered sugar.

Makes 4 servings.

1/3 c. milk
2 eggs, beaten
1 T. frozen orange juice concentrate, thawed
4 croissants, halved lengthwise
Garnish: powdered sugar

FAMILY-TIME CONVERSATION

The world's largest Christmas tree can be found in Indianapolis. The enormous tree is called the Circle of Lights and is decorated with 52 strands of garland and 4,784 lights.

CHAPTER TWO

SAND DUNE

Salads, Sides & Breads

**TOSS TOGETHER GREAT TASTE
AND HEALTHY GOODNESS
TO MAKE FRESH, SATISFYING
AND TASTY SALADS, SIDES
AND BREADS THAT ARE PACKED
WITH FULL-ON FLAVOR.**

TOMATO-GARBANZO SALAD

AUBREY DUFOUR
SALEM, IN

Try this tasty salad the next time you're looking for something new to tote to a get-together.

1 c. elbow macaroni, uncooked

15-oz. can garbanzo beans, drained and rinsed

2 c. tomatoes, diced

1 c. celery, diced

1/2 c. red onion, diced

1/3 c. olive oil

1/4 c. lemon juice

2 T. fresh parsley, chopped

2 t. ground cumin

2 t. salt

1/2 t. pepper

Cook macaroni according to package directions; drain and rinse in cold water. Transfer to a large bowl and combine with remaining ingredients. Stir to mix well. Cover and chill at least one hour.

Makes 6 servings.

PULL-APART BACON BREAD

DEB YOUNG
MILFORD, IN

A hearty burst of flavors...so good!

Heat oil in a large skillet; sauté green pepper and onion until tender. Remove from heat; set aside. Slice biscuits into quarters; place in a bowl. Add pepper mixture, bacon, margarine and cheese; toss until mixed. Transfer mixture to a greased 10" tube pan; bake at 350 degrees for 30 minutes. Invert onto a serving platter to serve.

Serves 8.

1 t. oil
3/4 c. green pepper, chopped
3/4 c. onion, chopped
3 7-1/2 oz. tubes refrigerated buttermilk biscuits
1 lb. bacon, crisply cooked and crumbled
1/4 c. margarine, melted
1 c. shredded Cheddar cheese

PIZZA PASTA SALAD

**AMBER BELT
BROOKSTON, IN**

This is our go-to potluck recipe. I like to bring something our children will eat, and they go gaga over this! If I'm bringing it to a cookout, they'll ask me to make extra to leave at home. This recipe is very forgiving, so feel free to swap out an ingredient or two.

12-oz. pkg. bowtie pasta, uncooked

14-1/2 oz. can petite diced tomatoes, drained

2/3 c. pepperoni, diced

2/3 c. salami, diced

1/2 c. shredded Parmesan cheese

1 c. shredded mozzarella cheese

1/2 to 1 c. Italian salad dressing

Cook pasta according to package directions; drain and rinse with cold water. Combine pasta and remaining ingredients in a serving bowl; toss gently until evenly mixed. Cover and refrigerate at least one hour before serving. If salad starts to get dry, add a little more salad dressing.

Serves 8 to 12.

SWEET-AND-SOUR CABBAGE SALAD

LAURA FULLER
FORT WAYNE, IN

This recipe has been in the family over 40 years. It's a favorite for get-togethers and potlucks.

Place cabbage in a large bowl with a lid; arrange onion slices over cabbage. Sprinkle with 1/2 cup sugar and set aside. In a small saucepan, combine remaining sugar and other ingredients. Bring to a rolling boil over medium heat; stir until sugar dissolves. Immediately pour over cabbage mixture. Cover and refrigerate overnight, stirring after 4 hours.

Serves 10 to 12.

1 head cabbage, shredded
3/4 c. onion, thinly sliced
1/2 c. plus 1 t. sugar, divided
1/3 c. oil
1/2 c. vinegar
1/2 t. dry mustard
1/2 t. celery seed
1/2 t. salt

PRESENTATION

Simple garnishes dress up main dishes all year 'round! Fresh mint sprigs add coolness and color to summertime dishes, while rosemary sprigs and cranberries add a festive touch to holiday platters.

GREEN GODDESS
BACON SALAD

JULIE ANN PERKINS
ANDERSON, IN

I grew up loving Green Goddess dressing, my grandmother used it all the time. We relished salads, especially when everything was fresh from the garden or readily available at the Main Street fruit market! The family-owned market is still there...how blessed we are.

7 eggs, hard-boiled, peeled and sliced

7 to 12 slices bacon, chopped and crisply cooked

3 c. deli roast chicken, shredded

6 to 8 c. baby spinach

1 red pepper, chopped

Optional: 1 bunch green onions, sliced

Green Goddess salad dressing to taste

In a large salad bowl, combine eggs, bacon, chicken and vegetables; mix well. Pass salad dressing at the table so guests may add it to taste.

Makes 6 servings

SOFT SESAME BREAD STICKS

LYNN WILLIAMS
MUNCIE, IN

These yummy bread sticks go great with soups or salads...I make plenty because they disappear quickly!

In a small bowl, combine flour, sugar, baking powder and salt. Gradually add milk; stir to form a soft dough. Turn onto a floured surface; knead gently 3 to 4 times. Roll into a 10-inch by 5-1/2 inch rectangle; cut into 12 bread sticks. Place butter in a 13"x9" baking pan; coat bread sticks in butter and sprinkle with sesame seed. Bake at 450 degrees for 14 to 18 minutes, until golden.

1-1/4 c. all-purpose flour
2 t. sugar
1-1/2 t. baking powder
1/2 t. salt
2/3 c. milk
2 T. butter, melted
2 t. sesame seed

Makes one dozen.

EFFIE'S BUTTER BEAN CASSEROLE

SUSAN SPARKS
KOKOMO, IN

This dish has been a family favorite since I was a little girl. We really looked forward to having Effie's casserole at our holiday meals! The sauce for this recipe can be made ahead of time and refrigerated or frozen, making it simple and fast if you need a quick side dish for dinner or a covered dish for a carry-in.

In a large skillet over medium heat, cook bacon until crisp. Cut bacon into small pieces; return to skillet. Stir in remaining ingredients except beans. Simmer over medium-low heat for 30 minutes. Add beans to a lightly greased 13"x9" baking pan; spoon sauce over beans. Bake, uncovered, at 375 degrees for one hour, or until hot and bubbly.

1/2 lb. bacon
1 c. onion, chopped
1 green pepper, chopped
1 c. brown sugar, packed
2 6-oz. cans tomato paste
3 c. water
2 t. steak sauce
1/8 t. garlic salt
4 16-oz. cans butter beans, drained

Serves 6 to 8.

LOADED BROCCOLI & CAULIFLOWER CASSEROLE

CYNTHIA KIMBLE
LOGANSPORT, IN

I started making this recipe for a family member who was practicing a keto diet. Everyone loves it and I am asked to make it quite often.

1/2 head cauliflower, cut into flowerets

1/2 bunch broccoli, cut into flowerets

8 slices bacon

1/2 c. sour cream

1/2 c. mayonnaise

1 T. whipping cream

1/4 t. pepper

1 c. shredded sharp Cheddar cheese

6 T. fresh chives, chopped and divided

1 c. shredded Colby & Monterey Jack cheese

In a large saucepan, bring 1/2-inch water to a boil over medium heat. Add cauliflower and broccoli. Cook for 10 to 15 minutes, until crisp-tender; drain. Meanwhile, cook bacon in a large skillet over medium heat until crisp. Drain; crumble and set aside. In a large bowl, combine sour cream, mayonnaise, cream and pepper. Add cauliflower, broccoli, Cheddar cheese, half of the bacon and half of the chives. Mix well; transfer to a 13"x9" baking pan sprayed with non-stick vegetable spray. Top with Colby & Monterey Jack cheese and remaining bacon and chives. Cover with aluminum foil. Bake at 370 degrees for 20 minutes. Remove foil; bake another 5 to 10 minutes, just until cheese is bubbly and beginning to turn golden.

Serves 8.

JAM MUFFINS

KATHY GRASHOFF
FORT WAYNE, IN

You probably already have the ingredients on hand to make a batch of these yummy muffins! Perfect for a snack or alongside soup.

In a large bowl, whisk together flour, sugar, baking powder and salt; set aside. In another bowl, whisk together egg, milk, melted butter and vanilla. Add egg mixture to flour mixture; stir until combined. Batter will be thick. Set aside 1/4 cup batter. Spoon remaining batter into 12 greased muffin cups, filling 1/3 full. Drop one teaspoon jam or preserves into each muffin cup; top each with one teaspoon remaining batter. (There's no need to cover the jam; you aren't trying to seal it in.) Bake at 400 degrees for 20 to 25 minutes, until a toothpick inserted near the center tests clean. Cool slightly; turn muffins out of pan and cool on a wire rack.

2-1/2 c. all-purpose flour
1/2 c. sugar
1 T. baking powder
1/2 t. salt
1 egg, beaten
1 c. milk
1/2 c. butter, melted
1 t. vanilla extract
1/4 c. favorite jam or preserves

Makes one dozen.

PICNIC PASTA SALAD

KELLYJEAN GETTELFINGER
SELLERSBURG, IN

Each summer, my entire family would drive 90 minutes to visit a local theme park together. We would all disperse within the park, then meet up later for a picnic lunch. I always brought this pasta salad. Every time I eat it, I think of our fun family picnics at the theme park. Serve and enjoy the picnic!

Cook pasta according to package directions; drain and rinse with cold water. Transfer pasta to a bowl; add half of the dressing. Add tomatoes and seasonings to taste; cover and chill. At serving time, more dressing may be added if pasta seems dry.

16-oz. pkg. linguine pasta, uncooked
20-oz. bottle Italian salad dressing, divided
2 ripe tomatoes, diced
salad seasoning and chili powder to taste

Makes 6 to 8 servings.

BROCCOLI PASTA SLAW

CAROLYN GOCHENAUR
HOWE, IN

One day, my sister and I saw this recipe on a TV cooking show. So we tried it and liked it a lot! Almonds and raisins make it festive for the holidays. I've been asked for the recipe several times.

8-oz. pkg. bowtie pasta, uncooked

16-oz. pkg. broccoli slaw

1 c. slivered almonds

1 c. dark or golden raisins

DRESSING

1 c. low-fat plain yogurt

1/2 c. mayonnaise

6 T. cider vinegar

2 T. sugar

1/4 to 1/2 t. cayenne pepper

salt and pepper to taste

Cook pasta according to package directions; drain. Rinse with cold water; drain again and place in a large bowl. Add slaw, almonds and raisins. Pour Dressing over pasta mixture; stir to coat. Serve immediately and refrigerate any leftovers.

Dressing:
Whisk together all ingredients until sugar dissolves.

Serves 6.

ANGEL HAIR PASTA SALAD

BARBARA KLEIN
NEWBURGH, IN

My sister-in-law Michele gave me this recipe and it has become a family favorite. I often take this to carry-in dinners and everyone loves it! The flavors mingle as it chills and it's just delicious.

Cook pasta according to package directions; drain. Rinse with cool water; drain and transfer to a large bowl. In a small bowl, mix together oil, lemon juice and salt; add to pasta and toss gently. Cover and refrigerate for 8 to 10 hours. Add remaining ingredients; mix well and chill until serving time.

Serves 10 to 12.

16-oz. pkg. angel hair pasta, uncooked

1/4 c. plus 1 T. oil

1/4 c. lemon juice

2-1/2 T. seasoned salt, or to taste

1-1/4 c. celery, sliced

2/3 c. green pepper, chopped

3/4 c. yellow onion, green onions or shallots, chopped

3/4 c. black olives, chopped

1 to 2 ripe tomatoes, diced

1-1/2 c. mayonnaise

MOLLY'S UN-TATER SALAD

MOLLY EBERT
COLUMBUS, IN

Since I was diagnosed with diabetes, I have to watch my carb intake. I tried several other recipes using cauliflower instead of potatoes but wasn't quite happy with the results. So I experimented until I finally came up with this delicious version. Even folks who think they don't like cauliflower love this!

2 16-oz. pkgs. frozen
cauliflower, thawed

3 eggs, hard-boiled,
peeled and diced

1/2 c. celery, sliced

1/2 c. green onions,
sliced

1/2 c. dill pickles, diced

Garnish: paprika

DRESSING

1/2 c. sour cream

1/4 c. plain Greek
yogurt

1/4 c. mayonnaise

1/2 t. salt

Steam cauliflower according to package directions, just until crisp-tender. Drain; cut cauliflower into bite-size pieces and place in a large salad bowl. Add remaining ingredients except paprika. Add Dressing; toss gently to coat all ingredients. Garnish with a sprinkle of paprika. Cover and chill several hours to allow flavors to blend.

Dressing:

Mix together all ingredients in a small bowl.

Makes 12 servings.

  Indiana – – – – – – – – – – – –

CHEESY HAM & CAULIFLOWER BAKE

MOLLY EBERT
COLUMBUS, IN

My guests gobble up this lighter version of scalloped potatoes! The cauliflower makes for a nice change from potatoes.

Arrange cauliflower in a lightly greased 11"x7" baking pan; top with ham. In a bowl, whisk together soup and milk until smooth; pour over ham. In a separate bowl, combine biscuit mix, butter, cheese and nutmeg. Mix until crumbly and sprinkle over soup mixture. Sprinkle with paprika. Bake, uncovered, at 400 degrees for 20 to 25 minutes, until topping is golden.

Makes 6 to 8 servings.

2 10-oz. pkg's. frozen cauliflower, thawed and well drained

1-1/4 c. cooked ham, cubed

10-3/4 oz. can Cheddar cheese soup

1/4 c. milk

2/3 c. biscuit baking mix

2 T. butter, softened

2 T. shredded Cheddar cheese

1/2 t. nutmeg

paprika to taste

KITCHEN TIP

A melon baller has lots of uses besides making juicy fruit salads. Put it to work forming perfect balls of cookie dough, coring apples and even making pretty little servings of butter for the dinner table. Clever!

EASY TRI-COLOR BEAN DISH

ERI NISKA
FORT WAYNE, IN

I came up with this recipe while looking in my pantry trying to come up with a quick side dish for dinner. The result was so yummy that I've made it over & over again.

15-oz. can cannellini beans, drained and rinsed

12-oz. jar fire-roasted red peppers, drained and diced

12-oz. jar marinated artichokes

In a saucepan over medium-low heat, combine beans, peppers and undrained artichokes. Gently heat through for about 5 minutes, until artichoke marinade is absorbed by beans and peppers. Serve warm, or cover and refrigerate for up to a week. Flavor will improve with time. May be reheated before serving, just until warm.

Makes 5 servings.

BARLEY CONFETTI SALAD

MOLLY EBERT
DECATUR, IN

My wonderful son-in-law is vegan. That has challenged me to come up with some new veggie dishes to serve when he comes to visit. This salad with its bold flavors is a big hit!

4 c. cooked barley

1/4 c. olive oil

3 T. lemon juice

2 cloves garlic, minced

1/2 c. fresh dill, chopped

2 c. tomatoes, diced

2 c. cucumbers, diced

1/2 c. green onions, sliced

salt and pepper to taste

In a large serving bowl, toss barley with olive oil, lemon juice and garlic. Stir in dill. Add tomatoes, cucumbers and green onions; mix gently. Season with salt and pepper. Cover and chill at least one hour to allow flavors to blend.

Makes 8 servings.

SPICY PARMESAN PASTA SALAD

JIMMY COX
WESTFIELD, IN

I made this recipe for my wife, Megan, in our first year of marriage, just experimenting. She loves spicy food, so her favorite part of the recipe is the crushed red pepper flakes. It's very good...give it a try!

Cook pasta according to package directions. Drain; rinse in cold water and drain again. Transfer pasta to a large bowl. Add peppers, pepperoni and 3/4 of salad dressing to pasta and mix. Add desired amount of red pepper flakes and mix. Add Parmesan cheese and mix. Cover and refrigerate for 4 or more hours. At serving time, add remaining salad dressing; toss to mix well.

Serves 15 to 20.

12-oz. pkg. tri-color rotini pasta, uncooked
1 red pepper, diced
1 orange pepper, diced
3-1/2 oz. pkg. pepperoni slices, quartered
16-oz. bottle zesty Italian salad dressing, divided
1/2 c. red pepper flakes, or to taste
1 c. grated Parmesan cheese

JUST FOR FUN

Elwood Haynes built one of the first automobiles in the US and successfully tested his one-horsepower, one-cylinder vehicle at 6 or 7 miles per hour on July 4, 1894, at Kokomo, Indiana. Haynes received the first U.S. traffic ticket when in 1895 a policeman on a bicycle ordered him and his automobile off the streets of Chicago.

CRISP SPINACH SALAD

CATHY BARR
LOGANSPORT, IN

We love this salad with grilled steak or pasta dishes.

2 bunches fresh spinach, torn and stems removed

2 cucumbers, peeled and diced

1 c. celery, sliced

1/2 c. pine nuts

1/2 c. black olives, quartered

1/2 c. green olives with pimentos, quartered

1/2 c. fresh flat-leaf parsley, minced

OLIVE OIL DRESSING

3/4 c. olive oil

1 t. salt

1/4 c. red wine vinegar

pepper to taste

1/8 t. dried oregano

Combine all ingredients in a large bowl. Drizzle with Olive Oil Dressing; toss to mix well.

Olive Oil Dressing:

Whisk or shake together all ingredients.

Makes 6 to 8 servings.

PAULETTE'S POTATO SALAD

PAULETTE DOWNTON
FRANKLIN, IN

Over the years I've tried several potato salad recipes, but I keep coming back to this one. It's tried & true.

In a large bowl, stir together mayonnaise, vinegar, sugar and seasonings. Add remaining ingredients; toss to coat well. Cover and chill for 2 hours before serving.

Makes 6 servings.

1 c. mayonnaise
2 T. white vinegar
1 t. sugar
1-1/2 t. salt
1/4 t. pepper
1 c. celery, sliced
1/2 c. onion, chopped
4 c. redskin potatoes, peeled, cubed and cooked
2 eggs, hard-boiled, peeled and chopped

SPECIAL GRILLED ZUCCHINI

KATIE BLACK
FREELANDVILLE, IN

Over the years we had to find a healthy way to eat all that zucchini everyone brought us! This is a yummy side dish, or enjoy it all by itself for a light summer meal.

Spray two 12-inch squares of heavy-duty aluminum foil generously with olive oil spray. Layer vegetables on foil in the order listed. Drizzle evenly with soy sauce. Fold foil loosely into packets. Grill over medium heat for about 10 minutes, until vegetables are tender.

Makes 2 to 4 servings.

1 to 2 zucchini, sliced
1 yellow squash, sliced
1/2 red onion, sliced
12 mushrooms, sliced
8 cherry tomatoes
2 T. light soy sauce

RANCH CORNBREAD SALAD

RUBY PRUITT
NASHVILLE, IN

I like taking different dishes to our church pitch-in dinners, and this one was a big hit! With its layered colors, this hearty salad looks very pretty in the clear glass bowl I use.

8-1/2 oz. pkg. cornbread mix
1 c. mayonnaise
1 c. sour cream
1-1/2 T. ranch salad dressing mix
16-oz. can pinto beans, drained
1/4 c. sweet onion, chopped
2 tomatoes, chopped
1 green, yellow or red pepper, chopped
16-oz. can corn, drained
1 lb. bacon, crisply cooked and crumbled
2 c. shredded Cheddar cheese

Prepare and bake cornbread mix according to package directions; let cool. Meanwhile, in a small bowl, mix together mayonnaise, sour cream and salad dressing mix; cover and refrigerate. Crumble cooled cornbread into a deep clear glass bowl. Layer with beans, onion, tomatoes, pepper, corn and bacon. Spread mayonnaise mixture over top; sprinkle with cheese. Serve immediately, or cover and chill until serving time.

Makes 10 servings.

MAPLE-GLAZED CARROTS

KATHY GRASHOFF
FORT WAYNE, IN

A quick-to-fix side that goes nicely with any main dish.

Place carrots in a saucepan and cover with water; bring to a boil over medium heat. Cook for 10 minutes, or until crisp-tender; drain. Set aside. Cook bacon in a skillet over medium heat for 3 minutes, or until lightly browned. Add apple and cook for 2 minutes. Add carrots, maple syrup, salt and pepper; stir frequently. Cook until carrots are warmed through and lightly glazed. Serve immediately.

16-oz. pkg. baby carrots
3 slices bacon, chopped
1 apple, peeled, cored and sliced into thin wedges
2 T. maple syrup
salt and pepper to taste

Serves 4.

FAMILY-TIME CONVERSATION

Paul Vories McNutt (July 19, 1891 – March 24, 1955) was an American diplomat and politician who served as the 34th governor of Indiana. McNutt ended Prohibition in Indiana. He also enacted Indiana's first income tax regime.

SWEET POTATO TOSS

**JANET MONNETT
CLOVERDALE, IN**

As my family and I were changing to a vegetarian diet, I tried to create dishes that everyone would find tasty. This is a delicious side dish that we all just love!

canola oil for frying
2 sweet potatoes, peeled
and sliced
4 potatoes, peeled and
sliced
1/2 to 1 T. onion powder
1/8 t. sugar
salt to taste

Into a skillet over medium-high heat, add oil to 1/2-inch depth. Combine all potato slices in a bowl; toss with seasonings. Add potatoes to hot oil in skillet. Cover and cook, turning as needed. Reduce heat to medium when potatoes begin to soften. Uncover for the last 3 to 4 minutes of cooking to crisp up potatoes.

Serves 4 to 6.

FAMILY-TIME CONVERSATION

The first and only known working rotary jail still exists today in Crawfordsville, Indiana. It was built in 1882 and served Montgomery County till 1972. The rotary jail is a space-saving innovation, very much like a revolving door at the mall. It saved officers from always having to physically deal with prisoners and instead "crank" the rotary jail to face the one single cell door to let prisoners out.

CARROTS AU GRATIN

CAROL SAGESER
GREENSBURG, IN

Delightfully easy and deliciously cheesy.

Place carrots in a saucepan. Cover with water and cook over medium heat until crisp-tender; drain. Combine carrots, soup and cheese in a one-quart casserole dish lightly sprayed with non-stick vegetable spray; set aside. Mix bread crumbs and butter; sprinkle over carrot mixture. Bake at 350 degrees for 20 to 25 minutes.

Serves 6.

3 c. carrots, peeled and sliced

10-3/4 oz. can cream of celery soup

1 c. shredded Cheddar cheese

1/4 c. dry bread crumbs

1 T. butter, melted

CREAM CHEESY MEXICAN CORN

**ANNE WELBORN
FORT WAYNE, IN**

This recipe brings memories of a time when I worked as a university resident director. When the students went home for Thanksgiving, several of us resident directors would stay to supervise those who remained on campus. The dean of residence life invited me to his family's home for Thanksgiving dinner so I would not have to spend it alone. This is the dish I took...it was a hit!

2 15-oz. cans corn, drained
1/2 red pepper, diced
1/2 green pepper, diced
8-oz. pkg. cream cheese, cubed

Combine all ingredients in a saucepan over medium-low heat. Cook, stirring occasionally, until cream cheese melts and peppers are cooked through.

Serves 6.

PRESENTATION

For an easy edible centerpiece for your garden party, cut floral shapes from your favorite rolled sugar cookie recipe. Add a long skewer-type stick and bake as directed. Decorate the cookies as desired and poke them into a prepared flowerpot. Your guests can then pick a "flower" for dessert.

HOPPIN' JOHN

CAROLINE WEINERT
BEDFORD, IN

It's said that eating Hoppin' John on New Year's Day will bring a prosperous year filled with luck. The black-eyed peas are symbolic of pennies or coins. This is an easy dish that my family really enjoys!

Cover peas with water and soak 8 hours to overnight; rinse and drain. Add 8 cups water to a large saucepan; bring to a boil. Add peas; boil for 2 minutes. Remove from heat; cover and let stand for one hour. Drain peas, reserving 6 cups of cooking water. In a Dutch oven over medium-high heat, cook bacon until crisp; remove from pan, reserving drippings. Drain bacon on paper towels. Add onion and garlic to Dutch oven; cook for one to 2 minutes, until tender. Stir in peas, rice, seasonings and reserved cooking water; bring to a boil. Cover and reduce heat. Simmer for one hour, stirring occasionally, until peas and rice are tender. Stir in bacon before serving.

1 c. dried black-eyed peas
8 c. water
6 slices bacon, chopped
3/4 c. onion, diced
1 clove garlic, minced
1 c. long-cooking rice, uncooked
2 t. salt
1/4 t. pepper

Serves 4 to 6.

CHAPTER THREE

SOUPER SPEEDWAY

Soups & Sandwiches

GATHER 'ROUND TOGETHER WITH

FAMILY & FRIENDS TO COZY UP

WITH A BOWL OF HEARTY SOUP OR

A TASTY SANDWICH PERFECT

FOR TAILGATING, CAMPFIRES

& GAME NIGHT!

PARTY-TIME LASAGNA BUNS

JOYCE STATH
TELL CITY, IN

Here's a hint to prevent the rolls from tearing...place them in the freezer for about an hour prior to slicing.

4 French bread rolls
1 lb. ground beef
1.35-oz. pkg. onion or
   mushroom soup mix
1/4 t. dried oregano
1/4 t. dried basil
8-oz. can tomato sauce
3/4 c. cottage cheese
2 c. shredded mozzarella
   cheese, divided

1 egg, beaten

Slice the top of each roll and set aside. Hollow out the rolls. In a skillet over medium heat, brown beef; drain. Stir in soup mix, seasonings and tomato sauce. Simmer until heated through. In a bowl, mix cottage cheese, one cup mozzarella and egg. For each sandwich, spoon a layer of the beef mixture into the bottom of a bun. Spoon on a layer of cheese mixture and a layer of beef mixture. Top with remaining mozzarella. Replace bun top and wrap in aluminum foil. Place on a baking sheet and bake at 400 degrees for 30 minutes, or until cheese is melted.

Makes 4 sandwiches.

REUBEN SANDWICH

LAURA FULLER,
FORT WAYNE, IN

The sandwich of all sandwiches!

3 slices deli corned beef
1 to 2 slices Swiss cheese
2 slices pumpernickel or
   dark rye bread
1/4 c. sauerkraut, well
   drained
1-1/2 T. Thousand Island
   salad dressing
3 T. butter

Arrange corned beef and cheese on one slice of bread. Heap with sauerkraut; drizzle with salad dressing. Add second bread slice. Melt butter in a cast-iron skillet over medium heat. Add sandwich; grill on both sides until golden and cheese melts.

Makes one sandwich.

PORK TENDERLOIN SANDWICH

LYNN WILLIAMS,
MUNCIE, IN

As Hoosiers from the heart, this tenderloin sandwich is always a tradition and a good luck charm that we eat on game day.

Place each slice of pork tenderloin between 2 pieces of sturdy plastic wrap; flatten the cutlet until it's about 1/4 inch thick. Beat eggs and milk together; whisk in seasonings. Place bread crumbs in a shallow bowl. Dip each flattened cutlet into seasoned milk-egg mixture and then into the bread crumbs, thoroughly coating cutlets with crumbs. Set breaded cutlets aside on a piece of parchment or wax paper. Heat oil in a large skillet until the oil is shimmering. Gently lower cutlets, one at a time, into hot oil, and fry until golden on each side, about 8 minutes per cutlet. Drain cutlets on paper towels. Preheat oven broiler, and set oven rack about 6 inches from the heat source. Spread Kaiser rolls open with the cut sides up, and broil until rolls are toasted and hot, about one minute. Top each roll with a fried cutlet; top each cutlet with desired garnish.

Makes 4 sandwiches.

4 4 oz. slices pork tenderloin, cut across the grain

1 egg, beaten

2 T. milk

1/4 t. garlic powder

1/4 t. onion powder

1/4 t. seasoned salt

1/4 t. dried marjoram

1 t. salt

1/4 t. ground pepper

1-1/2 c. bread crumbs

1/2 c. oil

4 Kaiser rolls, split

Garnish: mayonnaise, ketchup, mustard, lettuce, tomato, onion, pickle

HOT CHICKEN SLOW-COOKER SANDWICHES

BRENDA SMITH
MONROE, IN

I like to serve these at club meetings or card parties. Everyone always asks for the recipe!

28-oz. can cooked chicken

2 10-3/4-oz. cans cream of chicken soup

1/4 c. water

4 T. grated Parmesan cheese

7 slices bread, toasted and cubed

1/4 c. red pepper, chopped

24 dinner rolls, split

Combine all ingredients, except for dinner rolls, in a 5-quart slow cooker. Cover and cook on low setting for 3 hours. Serve on rolls. If using your electric pressure cooker for this recipe, secure the lid and turn the pressure release lever to Venting. Press the Slow Cook setting and set temperature as needed for medium.

Makes 24 mini-sandwiches.

HAM & CORN CHOWDER

MOLLY EBERT
COLUMBUS, IN

This is a simple yet rich and comforting soup to share on a rainy day... a delicious way to use some of that leftover holiday ham.

2 T. butter

1/2 c. onion, finely chopped

3 T. all-purpose flour

14-1/2 oz. can chicken broth

2 c. potatoes, peeled and diced

2 15-oz. cans corn

2 c. half-and-half

1-1/2 c. cooked ham, diced

2 T. fresh parsley, snipped

Melt butter in a large saucepan over medium heat. Add onion and cook until tender, stirring frequently. Add flour; stir to make a paste. Slowly whisk in broth, stirring until smooth; add potatoes. Cover and cook for 10 minutes, or until potatoes are just tender. Stir in undrained corn and half-and-half. Reduce heat to low. Simmer, uncovered, for 6 to 8 minutes. Stir in ham and parsley; heat through but do not allow to boil.

Makes 8 servings.

PULLED PORK SANDWICHES

**LYNN WILLIAMS
MUNCIE, IN**

*We usually make this pulled pork for sandwiches, but sometimes we use it
for tacos, burritos, or on warm lettuce salads. It is good any way you use it!*

On your preassure cooker, select Sauté setting and add oil. Add pork and sear on both sides, for about 8 minutes total. Add onion and sauté for another 2 minutes. Press the Cancel function to reset cooker. Add broth, tomato paste, lemon juice, salt, pepper and paprika; stir well. Secure the lid and set pressure release to Sealing. Select Manual/Pressure and cook on high pressure for 45 minutes. Once cooking is complete, let the pressure release naturally for 10 minutes. Release any remaining pressure manually using the Venting/Quick Release method. Open cooker; transfer the pork to a plate. Shred pork and return to cooker. Select Sauté and cook for 5 minutes more to reduce liquid. Press Cancel to reset cooker. Remove pork from cooker and serve on toasted buns.

3 T. olive oil
2 lbs. pork shoulder, fat
  trimmed
1/2 c. onion, chopped
1 c. chicken broth
1/2 c. tomato paste
1 T. lemon juice
1 t. salt
1 t. pepper
1 t. smoked paprika
toasted buns split

Serves 8.

DINNERTIME CONVERSATION

On May 30, 1911, at the Indianapolis Motor Speedway, the first long-distance auto race in the U. S. was hosted. The 200-lap Indianapolis 500 is still held there every Memorial Day weekend at Indiana.

SIMMERED KIELBASA & CABBAGE SOUP

AGNELINE HAVERSTOCK
LA PORTE, IN

We go camping in Brown County in central Indiana every fall. We put this soup in the slow cooker before we start sightseeing for the day. It really hits the spot when we return!

1/2 head cabbage, chopped

2 potatoes, peeled and diced

2 carrots, peeled and diced

1 onion, chopped

Optional: 2 to 4 cloves garlic, minced

1/2 lb. Kielbasa sausage, diced

1 T. red wine vinegar

3 T. fresh dill, finely chopped

1 bay leaf

salt and pepper to taste

6 c. beef or chicken broth

Layer all ingredients in a slow cooker in order listed. Cover and cook on low setting for 5 to 6 hours. At serving time, stir well; discard bay leaf.

Makes 4 to 6 servings.

DINNERTIME CONVERSATION

Hoosier Hill in Wayne County is the highest point in Indiana. It is at 1,257 feet above sea level. Posey County, where the Wabash River meets the Ohio River, is the lowest point.

CORN CHOWDER WITH BACON

TINA VAWTER
SHERIDAN, IN

A chilly-weather family favorite that's one of our comfort foods. Sometimes I'll add a little extra bacon...can't have too much!

Cook bacon in a Dutch oven over medium heat until almost crisp. Add onion and cook until tender; drain drippings, if desired. Add chicken broth, corn and potatoes; cover and bring to a boil. Reduce heat to medium-low. Simmer 12 to 15 minutes, until potatoes are tender. Add salt and pepper to taste; garnish with parsley.

Serves 8.

8 slices bacon, diced
1 c. onion, chopped
4 14-1/2 oz. cans chicken broth
4 c. creamed corn
4 c. potatoes, peeled and diced
salt and pepper to taste
Garnish: chopped fresh parsley

EGGSTRA SPECIAL BLT

LISA SANDERS
SHOALS, IN

A wonderful way to celebrate that first ripe red tomato from the garden. You'll want to have plenty of napkins handy!

Fry egg in butter as desired; season with salt and pepper. Flip egg; top with cheese slice and let melt. On toasted bread, layer lettuce, onion, tomato, bacon and cheese-topped egg. Spread mayonnaise on remaining slice of toast; close sandwich.

Makes one sandwich.

1 egg
1 to 2 t. butter
salt and pepper to taste
1 slice favorite cheese
2 slices bread, toasted
1 to 2 leaves ruffled lettuce
1 thin slice onion
1 slice ripe tomato
3 to 4 slices cooked bacon
Garnish: mayonnaise

HEARTY SAUSAGE SOUP

DARLA COTTOM
TERRE HAUTE, IN

My boys loved this slow-cooker soup when they were little. Use your own judgment on the amount of spaghetti to make it as thick or as soupy or as you want. Caution...a little goes a long way!

1 lb. ground pork sausage
1 green pepper, diced
1 onion, diced
1/3 of a 16-oz. pkg. angel hair pasta, uncooked and broken into 2-inch pieces
28-oz. can diced tomatoes
14-1/2 oz. can diced tomatoes
12-oz. can tomato juice
garlic salt to taste
1/8 t. sugar

Brown sausage in a skillet over medium heat. Drain; transfer to a 5-quart slow cooker. Add green pepper and onion; place desired amount of spaghetti pieces on top of vegetables. Add tomatoes with juice and remaining ingredients. Cover and cook on low setting for 4 to 6 hours.

Makes 6 to 8 servings.

JUST FOR FUN

There is a road in Amity, Indiana, with a gravesite in the middle of it. In 1831, Nancy Kerlin Barnett was buried overlooking Sugar Creek, but plans to build a road through the site meant that the bodies had to be moved. Barnett's grandson guarded her grave with a shotgun while the others were moved. County officials eventually agreed to let it be, building the road around the plot. The concrete slab protecting the grave and historical marker were added later.

FRENCH MARKET SOUP

DEBBY MARCUM
GOSPORT, IN

This soup is wonderful to enjoy while watching a Sunday night football game! I love to simmer mine all afternoon for the flavors to really develop. Be sure to serve it with a dollop of sour cream and some warm crusty bread. It's even better the next day!

In a large soup pot, combine all ingredients except garnish, adding seasoning packet from beans. (There's no need to soak beans or brown meats.) Bring to a boil over high heat; reduce heat to medium-low. Simmer for 2-1/2 to 3 hours, stirring occasionally, until beans are soft. Garnish servings with a dollop of sour cream.

Makes 8 to 10 servings.

20-oz. pkg. 15-bean soup mix, rinsed and sorted
1 lb. boneless, skinless chicken breasts, chopped
1 lb. smoked pork sausage, sliced
1 lb. cooked ham, diced
14-1/2 oz. can diced tomatoes
8 c. water
1 onion, finely chopped
1 clove garlic, minced
1/4 t. dried oregano
1/4 t. cinnamon
1/2 t. salt
Garnish: sour cream

BIG GAME SLOPPY JOES

**LAURA FULLER
FORT WAYNE, IN**

*Popular at all our football get-togethers! If you prefer, use ground turkey,
or a mix of beef and turkey.*

2 T. olive oil

1 c. onion, coarsely
chopped

1 red or yellow pepper,
coarsely chopped

1-1/2 lbs. ground beef or
turkey

2 to 3 cloves garlic,
chopped

2 T. chili powder

1/2 t. dry mustard

1 t. salt

1/2 t. pepper

12-oz. bottle regular or
non-alcoholic beer

6-oz. can tomato paste

3 T. light brown sugar,
packed

1 T. Worcestershire
sauce

6 hamburger buns, split
and toasted

Press the sauté button on a 5-quart electric pressure
cooker. Add oil, onion and red or yellow pepper;
cook for about 2 minutes, until softened. Add beef or
turkey and garlic. Cook, stirring occasionally, until no
longer pink; drain. Stir in seasonings; cook for one to
2 minutes. Add remaining ingredients except buns;
stir well. Close and lock the lid. Set heat to high; turn
as low as possible once high pressure is reached.
Set timer and cook for 5 minutes. Open pressure
cooker using quick release method. Serve beef
mixture spooned onto buns.

Serves 6.

PRESENTATION

Set up a framed menu to let everyone
know that delicious dishes like Great
Grandmother's Pot Roast and Aunt
Betty's Pudding Cake await!

LOADED BAKED POTATO SOUP

BETH FLACK
TERRE HAUTE, IN

I like to serve this delicious soup with a loaf of crusty bread on cool fall evenings. Save out a little of the bacon and chives to garnish each bowl, if you like.

Add butter to a 5-quart slow cooker on high setting. When butter melts, add onion, celery and seasonings. Stir; let cook for several minutes. Add potatoes, garlic and broth. Turn slow cooker to low setting; cover and cook for 7 to 8 hours. Remove 1/4 cup of potatoes to a small bowl and mash; return to slow cooker. Stir in remaining ingredients; cover and cook for one additional hour.

Serves 6.

1/4 c. butter, sliced

1 onion, finely chopped

2 stalks celery, chopped

1 t. salt

1-1/2 t. pepper

8 russet potatoes, peeled and cut into 1/2-inch cubes

1 t. garlic, minced

2 14-oz. cans chicken broth

8-oz. container sour cream

8-oz. container whipping cream

8-oz. pkg. shredded Cheddar cheese

20-oz. pkg. real bacon crumbles

1/4 c. fresh chives, chopped

CAROLYN'S GOULASH

**CAROLYN GOCHENAUR
HOWE, IN**

*This is my go-to recipe in wintertime for feeding a big group. Everyone
loves it...it never lets me down!*

1 c. elbow macaroni,
 uncooked
3 lbs. ground beef
1/2 to 1 onion, diced
1/2 to 1 green pepper,
 diced
14-1/2 oz. can petite
 diced tomatoes
14-1/2 oz. can crushed
 tomatoes
2 10-3/4 oz. cans tomato
 soup
15-oz. can tomato sauce
15-1/4 oz. can corn,
 drained
1/2 c. catsup
2 T. cider vinegar
1 T. sugar
salt and pepper to taste
8-oz. pkg. shredded
 Cheddar cheese

Cook macaroni according to package directions;
drain and set aside. Meanwhile, in a large skillet
over medium heat, brown beef with onion and green
pepper; drain. Reduce heat to medium-low; simmer
for 15 to 20 minutes. Stir in tomatoes with juice and
remaining ingredients except cheese. Transfer beef
mixture to a greased deep 13"x9" baking pan; add
cooked macaroni and mix gently. Sprinkle cheese on
top. Bake, uncovered, at 350 degrees for 30 to
40 minutes, until bubbly and heated through.

Makes 15 servings.

KITCHEN TIP

A new twist on casserole toppers...
try crushed veggie, chicken or
cheese-flavored crackers combined
with fresh or dried herbs and melted
butter. Sprinkle on top before
baking for a delicious crunch.

SPICY SLIDERS

BETH FLACK
TERRE HAUTE, IN

Make these for an easy, quick school night dinner, tailgating party or appetizer at Christmas. This makes two pans, enough for a hungry crowd! But it's simple to halve the recipe for a smaller gathering.

Cook sausage and beef in a large skillet over medium heat, stirring until crumbled and no longer pink. Drain well; add tomatoes with juice and cheese. Cook for about 8 minutes, stirring often, until well blended and cheese is melted. Arrange bottom halves of 12 buns in each of 2 lightly greased 13"x9" baking pans. Spoon sausage mixture onto bun bottoms; add bun tops. Brush buns with melted butter. Bake, uncovered, at 350 degrees for about 12 minutes, until heated through.

Makes 2 dozen.

1 lb. hot ground pork sausage

1 lb. ground beef chuck

2 10-oz. cans diced tomatoes with green chiles

16-oz. pkg. pasteurized process cheese, cubed

24 slider buns, split

1/4 c. butter, melted

CAMP-OUT CHILI DOGS

KATHY GRASHOFF
FORT WAYNE, IN

I'm always looking for something easy to take to the lake. When it's too hot to grill, we'd much rather be relaxing in the water!

Place hot dogs in a slow cooker. In a bowl, combine chili, onion and chili powder; stir well and pour over hot dogs. Cover and cook on low setting for 4 to 6 hours, or on high setting for 1-1/2 to 2 hours. Add cheese just before serving; allow to melt slightly. Serve each hot dog in a roll with some chili spooned over top.

Serves 6 to 8.

1 lb. hot dogs

2 15-oz. cans chili with beans

1 onion, finely chopped

1 t. chili powder

1 c. shredded Cheddar cheese

8 hot dog rolls, split

CHAPTER FOUR

MONON TRAIL

Mains

FILL THEM UP WITH A STICK-TO-
THE-RIBS MEAL THAT IS FULL
OF FLAVOR AND HEARTY
ENOUGH TO SATISFY EVEN THE
BIGGEST APPETITE.

CHILI CHICKEN TACOS

BETH FLACK
TERRE HAUTE, IN

A family favorite...easy to make in your slow cooker. Serve Mexican rice on the side along with chips and salsa or queso.

2 lbs. boneless, skinless chicken breasts

1-1/4 oz. pkg. taco seasoning mix

1 T. brown sugar, packed

4-1/2 oz. can chopped green chiles

1 c. canned corn, drained

10-oz. can enchilada sauce

4 green onions, chopped

4.7-oz. pkg. corn taco shells

Garnish: shredded Mexican-blend cheese, shredded lettuce, chopped tomato, sour cream

Place chicken in a 5-quart slow cooker. Sprinkle with taco seasoning and brown sugar. Add chiles and corn; spoon enchilada sauce over all. Cover and cook on low setting for 6 to 7 hours; add onions during the last 15 minutes of cooking. Shred chicken with 2 forks; stir back into mixture in slow cooker. Meanwhile, bake taco shells according to package directions. Serve chicken mixture in taco shells with desired toppings.

Makes 6 servings.

QUICK BEEFY BEAN & BISCUIT BAKE

HANA BROSMER
HUNTINGBURG, IN

Golden biscuits layered over a hearty filling make this meal satisfying.

In a skillet over medium heat, brown beef with onion, salt and pepper; drain. Stir in baked beans, barbecue sauce and catsup; spoon beef mixture into an ungreased 13"x9" baking pan. Sprinkle cheese evenly over top. Separate each biscuit into 2 thinner biscuits and arrange evenly on top. Bake, uncovered, at 350 degrees for 30 to 35 minutes, until bubbly and biscuits are golden.

Makes 6 to 8 servings.

1 lb. ground beef
1/2 c. onion, chopped
1 t. salt
1/2 t. pepper
28-oz. can brown
  sugar baked beans
1/4 c. barbecue sauce
1/4 c. catsup
1 c. shredded Cheddar
  cheese
16.3-oz. tube
  refrigerated
  buttermilk biscuits

CHEESY CHILI CASSEROLE

DEANNA SANFORD
INDIANAPOLIS, IN

Comfort food from childhood! This was the first recipe I learned how to make. My mom helped me with the oven. I love this on cold rainy nights, plus it's so easy to toss together after a long day.

Layer chili, corn and cheese in a greased 8"x8" baking pan. Top with crushed tortilla chips. Bake, uncovered, at 350 degrees for 20 minutes, or until heated through and cheese is melted.

Serves 4.

2 14-1/2 oz. cans chili
15-1/4 oz. can corn
8-oz. pkg. shredded
  Cheddar cheese
1 to 1-1/2 c. tortilla
  chips, crushed

BEEF & BEAN TOSTADAS

KRISTA MARSHALL
FORT WAYNE, IN

Kids will love this crunchy eat-with-your-hands supper. Tostadas are like an open-faced taco...great for Mexican-themed parties!

1 lb. ground beef
1/2 c. onion, finely diced
1-1/4 oz. pkg. taco seasoning mix
1 c. water
15-oz. can nacho cheese sauce
15-oz. can refried beans
6 corn tostada shells
Garnish: pico de gallo or salsa

Brown beef and onion in a skillet over medium heat; drain. Add taco seasoning and water; cook, stirring occasionally, for 5 to 7 minutes, until thickened. Meanwhile, place cheese sauce and beans in separate microwave-safe bowls. Heat, stirring occasionally, until warmed through. Spread tostada shells evenly with beans; top each with about 1/4 cup beef mixture. Drizzle with cheese sauce; garnish with pico de gallo or salsa.

Serves 6.

HAMBURGER STROGANOFF CASSEROLE

PAMELA BERRY
HUNTINGTON, IN

This casserole is a huge hit whenever I put it on the table.

16-oz. pkg. wide egg noodles, uncooked
2 lbs. ground beef
1 onion, chopped
10-3/4 oz. can low-fat cream of mushroom soup
8-oz. container sour cream
salt and pepper to taste

Cook noodles according to package directions; drain. Meanwhile, brown beef and onion in a large skillet over medium heat; drain. Mix soup and sour cream into beef mixture; add noodles. Season with salt and pepper. Spoon into a lightly greased 13"x9" baking pan. Bake, uncovered, at 350 degrees for 30 minutes, or until heated through.

Serves 8 to 10.

YUMMA-SETTA

LYNDA MCKINNEY
NORMAN, IN

I received this recipe years ago through a recipe chain letter. It was a keeper! Serve with tossed salad and cornbread or garlic bread.

Cook noodles according to package directions. Drain; stir chicken soup into noodles. Meanwhile, in a large skillet over medium heat, brown beef with onion, brown sugar, salt and pepper. Drain; stir tomato soup into beef mixture. In a greased 3-quart casserole dish, layer half of beef mixture, half of noodle mixture and half of cheese. Repeat layers, ending with cheese. Bake, uncovered, at 350 degrees for 30 minutes, or until bubbly and heated through.

Makes 6 to 8 servings.

16-oz. pkg. wide egg noodles, uncooked

10-3/4 oz. can cream of chicken soup

2 lbs. ground beef

1/4 c. onion, chopped

1 t. brown sugar, packed

salt and pepper to taste

10-3/4 oz. can tomato soup

8-oz. pkg. pasteurized process cheese, shredded, divided

BACON CHEESEBURGER PIZZA

CAROLYN DECKARD
BEDFORD, IN

This pizza is one of my grandkids' favorites. I always keep everything on hand to make this pizza when they come for a visit.

10-oz. tube refrigerated pizza dough
1/2 lb. lean ground beef
1/2 c. onion, chopped
8-oz. can pizza sauce
1 tomato, thinly sliced
2 slices bacon, crisply cooked and crumbled
1 c. shredded Cheddar cheese or diced American cheese

Unroll pizza dough according to package directions. Place on a greased baking sheet; build up edges slightly. Bake at 425 degrees for 8 to 10 minutes, until lightly golden. Meanwhile, in a large skillet over medium heat, cook beef and onion until beef is browned and onion is tender. Drain well. Spread pizza sauce over hot crust; spoon beef mixture over sauce. Top with tomato slices and bacon pieces; sprinkle with cheese. Bake at 425 degrees for about 10 minutes, or until sauce is bubbly and cheese is melted. Let stand several minutes; cut into squares.

Makes 4 servings.

GOODE & HEALTHY "FRIED" CHICKEN

CRIS GOODE
MOORESVILLE, IN

This very simple recipe gives you all the deliciousness of real fried chicken without all the fat and calories. Don't be fooled, though... we rarely have leftovers of this family favorite!

3 egg whites
2 to 3 c. panko bread crumbs
salt and pepper to taste
10 chicken thighs, skin removed

Beat egg whites in a shallow dish; set aside. Combine bread crumbs, salt and pepper in a gallon-size plastic zipping bag. Coat chicken with egg whites, one piece at a time. Drop chicken into bag and shake to coat lightly. Arrange chicken in two 13"x9" baking pans coated with non-stick vegetable spray. Bake, uncovered, at 350 degrees for 30 to 40 minutes, until chicken juices run clear.

Makes 10 servings.

Baja Bites, p108

Whether you are looking for a quick-to-make breakfast dish to start the day off right, no-fuss party fare for those special guests, satisfying soups and sandwiches for the perfect lunch, main dishes to bring them to the table fast, or a sweet little something to savor at the end of the meal, you'll love these recipes from the amazing cooks in beautiful Indiana.

Crabby Artichoke Spread, p112

Busy-Morning Banana Bread, p8

Pork & Apple Bites, p117

Cream Cheese-Filled Cupcakes, p126

Southern Veggie Brunch Casserole, p9

Quick Beefy Bean & Biscuit Bake, p77

Tomato-Garbonzo Salad, p38

Pork Tenderloin Sandwich, p63

Krista's Breakfast Tacos, p13

Soft Sesame Bread Sticks, p43

Peanut Butter French Toast, p12

Marble Cheesecake, p130

Raspberry Custard Pie, p127

Party-Time Lasagna Buns, p62

Pull-Apart Bacon Bread, p39

Green Goddess Bacon Salad, p42

Steak and Egg Hash, p15

Beef & Bean Tostadas, p78

Supreme Caramel Apple Rolls, p133

Mom's One-Pot Pork Chop Dinner, p87

Hot Chicken Slow-Cooker Sandwiches, p64

Pulled Pork Sandwiches, p65

GARLIC & PARMESAN BAKED CHICKEN

ANN DAVIS
BROOKVILLE, IN

Topped with Havarti cheese, this chicken is mouthwatering!

Combine 1/4 cup melted butter and garlic powder in a bowl; set aside. In a separate bowl, combine bread crumbs, cheese, parsley, salt and pepper. Dip chicken, one piece at a time, into butter mixture, then into crumb mixture. Arrange chicken in an ungreased 13"x9" baking pan. Drizzle remaining butter into pan. Bake, uncovered, at 375 degrees for 35 to 40 minutes, until chicken juices run clear. Remove from oven; immediately top each piece of chicken with a slice of cheese. Let stand for a few minutes, until cheese melts.

Serves 6.

1/2 c. butter, melted and divided
2 t. garlic powder
1/2 c. dry bread crumbs
1/4 c. grated Parmesan cheese
2 T. fresh parsley, chopped
1/4 t. salt
1/2 t. pepper
6 boneless, skinless chicken breasts
6 slices Havarti cheese

MOM'S ONE-POT PORK CHOP DINNER

KIM ALLEN
NEW ALBANY, IN

A dinner classic for good reason! Simple to prepare and so comforting.

Melt butter in a skillet over medium heat; brown pork chops for 3 to 5 minutes on each side. Add potatoes, carrots and onion to skillet. In a bowl, combine soup and water; add to skillet. Cover and simmer for 15 to 20 minutes, until vegetables are tender.

Makes 4 servings.

1 T. butter
4 pork chops
3 potatoes, peeled and sliced
2 c. baby carrots
1 onion, sliced
10-3/4 oz. can cream of mushroom soup
1/4 c. water

SWEET SAUSAGES & CABBAGE

CAROLYN DECKARD
BEDFORD, IN

You will want to double this recipe, it's so good! In the summertime, we always use fresh cabbage out of our garden.

4 sweet Italian pork sausage links

2 to 3 potatoes, peeled and quartered

4 c. green cabbage, finely sliced

1/2 c. water

Garnish: mustard, vinegar

Place sausages in a large skillet; arrange potatoes around sausages. Top with cabbage; add water. Cover and cook over low heat for 30 minutes, or until sausages are browned and potatoes are tender. Serve with mustard and vinegar.

Makes 4 servings.

SUPREME CHUCK ROAST

SANDY WARD
ANDERSON, IN

Such a nice dish to cozy up to on a cold, wintry night! Tender and delicious, an elegant meal. Serve with mashed potatoes, steamed vegetables and warm bread.

3 to 4-lb. beef chuck roast

1/2 c. brown sugar, packed

14-oz. bottle catsup

salt and pepper to taste

14-oz. can beef broth

Place roast in a Dutch oven or a roasting pan with a lid; set aside. Mix remaining ingredients in a bowl; spoon over roast. Cover and bake at 325 degrees for 3 hours, or until roast is very tender. Remove roast to a platter; slice and serve.

Makes 6 to 8 servings.

LEMONY PARM PASTA

LAURA FULLER
FORT WAYNE, IN

*I love to cook and bake, and have been doing so for well over 50 years.
As a working mother of five boys, all in sports, I definitely needed
something quick & easy to feed my family.*

Cook pasta according to package directions; drain.
Meanwhile, in a large skillet over medium heat,
sauté garlic in butter until tender. Add broccoli,
yellow pepper, lemon juice and zest, salt and pepper.
Cook for 3 to 5 minutes, until broccoli is crisp-tender.
Add cooked pasta to skillet; toss to coat. Top with
Parmesan cheese, if desired.

Makes 6 servings.

8-oz. cooked penne pasta

2 cloves garlic, minced

2 T. butter

10-oz. pkg. frozen
chopped broccoli,
thawed

1 yellow pepper, diced

3 T. lemon juice

2 t. lemon zest

1/2 t. salt

1/4 t. pepper

Optional: grated
Parmesan cheese

ENCHILADA-STUFFED POBLANOS

CAROLYN DECKARD
BEDFORD, IN

*My son-in-laws love this spicy recipe! We make them on the grill
when camping, and bake in the oven for our family cookouts.
Either way, it's a winner.*

2-1/2 c. cooked chicken, shredded

15-oz. can black beans, drained and rinsed

11-oz. can corn, drained

10-oz. can diced tomatoes and green chiles, drained

10-oz. can enchilada sauce

2 c. shredded Mexican-blend cheese, divided

1 t. salt

6 poblano peppers, halved lengthwise and seeded

In a large bowl, combine chicken, beans, corn, tomatoes, enchilada sauce, 1-1/2 cups cheese and salt. Fill pepper halves evenly with chicken mixture. Wrap each half loosely in aluminum foil. Grill over medium-high heat for about 20 minutes, until heated through and peppers are tender. Unwrap; sprinkle with remaining cheese and let stand several minutes, until cheese is melted. Unwrapped peppers may also be placed cut-side up In 2 lightly greased 13"x9" baking pans. Bake, uncovered, at 350 degrees for 30 minutes; sprinkle with remaining cheese. Return to oven for 5 minutes, or until cheese is melted.

Makes 12 servings.

PINEAPPLE-ORANGE GLAZED HAM

CAROLYN DECKARD
BEDFORD, IN

This is a great way to fix a ham for family gatherings. With a slow cooker, it's really simple. Everyone always wants my recipe!

Place ham in a 5-quart slow cooker. Pour reserved pineapple juice over ham; refrigerate pineapple. In a small bowl, combine brown sugar, one tablespoon marmalade and mustard; mix well and spread over ham. Cover and cook on low setting for 6 to 8 hours. About 5 minutes before serving, in a small microwave-safe bowl, combine pineapple and remaining marmalade; mix well. Microwave on high for 1-1/2 minutes, or until heated through, stirring once halfway through cooking. Remove ham from slow cooker; place on a cutting board. Slice ham and serve with pineapple mixture.

Serves 8 to 10.

3 to 5-lb. boneless cooked ham

8-oz. can crushed pineapple in unsweetened juice, drained and juice reserved

1/2 c. brown sugar, packed

3 T. orange marmalade, divided

1 t. mustard

DINNERTIME CONVERSATION

Whitewater, White, Blue, Wabash, St. Joseph and Maumee are the major rivers. The Wabash River is the longest free-flowing river east of the Mississippi River. It is the official river of Indiana.

SKILLET RAVIOLI WITH SPINACH

KATHY GRASHOFF
FORT WAYNE, IN

This dish is so easy and goes together quickly, using just a skillet. Be warned...it may only serve 2 to 3 people, it is that good! A crisp salad and crusty bread or garlic bread rounds it out.

1 T. olive oil

2 cloves garlic, chopped

5-oz. pkg. baby spinach

1/2 t. salt, divided

pepper or red pepper flakes to taste

18-oz. pkg. refrigerated cheese & spinach ravioli, uncooked

1/2 c. water

6 T. mascarpone cheese

1/2 c. grated Parmesan cheese

In an oven-proof skillet over medium-high heat, heat oil with garlic. Cook until garlic is barely golden, about 30 seconds to one minute. Add spinach and 1/4 teaspoon salt; cook for 3 to 4 minutes, until spinach is wilted. Season with pepper or red pepper flakes; transfer to a bowl and set aside. Add uncooked ravioli, water and remaining salt to same skillet. Bring to a boil over high heat; reduce heat to medium. Cover and cook for 3 to 5 minutes, until ravioli is heated through and tender. Add small spoonfuls of mascarpone cheese around ravioli; season with more salt and pepper. Return spinach to pan; sprinkle with Parmesan cheese. Heat a broiler rack 6 inches from heat; broil for 3 to 6 minutes, until ravioli is browned in spots. Serve immediately.

Serves 3 to 4.

PRESENTATION

Make it easy for guests to mingle and chat...set up food at several tables instead of one big party buffet. Place hot foods on one table, chilled foods on another, sweets on yet another.

CHICKEN TETRAZZINI

**CARMEN HYDE
SPENCERVILLE, IN**

This recipe is fairly simple. We've also made Turkey Tetrazzini with leftovers after the holidays. I hope your family enjoys it as much as ours does.

Cook spaghetti according to package directions; drain and return to pan. Meanwhile, in a large saucepan over medium heat, melt 3/4 cup butter. Sprinkle flour over butter; cook and stir until blended. Reduce heat to low. Add milk; cook and stir until thickened. Stir in garlic powder and soup; blend in cheese and chicken. Add chicken mixture to cooked spaghetti; mix well. Transfer mixture to a lightly greased 17"x11" baking pan. Melt remaining butter and combine with cracker crumbs; sprinkle on top. Bake, uncovered, at 350 degrees for 30 minutes, or until hot and bubbly.

Serves 10 to 12.

16-oz. pkg. thin spaghetti, uncooked and broken into 3 to 4 pieces

3/4 c. plus 2 T. butter, divided

1 c. all-purpose flour

4 c. milk

1 t. garlic powder

2 10-3/4 oz. cans cream of chicken soup

3 c. shredded Cheddar cheese

4 c. cooked chicken, chopped

12 buttery round crackers, crushed

SPARERIBS & SAUERKRAUT

PEGGY FRAZIER
INDIANAPOLIS, IN

This is definitely a comfort meal and one of our family favorites.
Our family enjoys this with buttered mashed potatoes, spooning the
sauerkraut on top of the mashed potatoes.

**6 to 7 lbs. country-style
pork loin spareribs,
cut into serving-size
portions**

salt and pepper to taste

**3 16-oz. cans sauerkraut,
very well drained**

**1-1/2 c. Granny Smith
apples, peeled, cored
and chopped**

**3/4 c. onion, coarsely
chopped**

8 to 12 whole cloves

**1/4 c. brown sugar,
packed**

1/4 t. pepper

**1-1/2 c. chicken broth, or
more as needed**

Arrange spareribs in a shallow roasting pan; season on all sides with salt and pepper. Broil under a preheated broiler, 6 inches from heat, for 20 to 30 minutes, until ribs are browned on all sides. In a heavy, deep Dutch oven, combine remaining ingredients; stir gently. Arrange ribs on top, pushing them down into sauerkraut mixture. Turn oven to 325 degrees; cover and bake for 2 hours. Baste twice, spooning up pan juices onto ribs. Make sure the liquid does not cook away; if it gets low, add more broth. (This will not be a problem if a heavy pan is used.) Serve sauerkraut mixture alongside ribs.

Makes 6 to 8 servings.

MILLIE'S SPEEDY SUPPER

BARBARA IMLER
NOBLESVILLE, IN

This is a recipe from my childhood that my working mother could put on the table quickly, so we had it often. It's still one of my favorite comfort foods. While it's simmering, make some mashed potatoes and a lettuce salad to go with it. A complete meal ready to serve in half an hour!

In a bowl, combine beef, oats, egg, garlic salt and pepper. Mix well with your hands. Form into golfball-size balls and flatten into patties. Add patties to a skillet over medium heat. Cook without turning, until very well browned; turn and cook other side. Remove patties to a plate. Drain skillet, reserving 2 tablespoons drippings. Add onions to reserved drippings; reduce heat to medium-low. Cook until onions start to soften but not brown, about 4 minutes. Stir in catsup, vinegar, sugar and salt; return patties to skillet. Simmer for 5 minutes. Serve patties and onion gravy from skillet with mashed potatoes.

Makes 4 servings.

1 lb. ground beef chuck
1/2 c. old-fashioned oats, uncooked
1 egg, beaten
1/2 t. garlic salt
1/4 t. pepper
3 onions, coarsely chopped
1-1/2 c. catsup
1/3 c. vinegar
1 t. sugar
1/2 t. salt
mashed potatoes

HAM, BACON, CABBAGE & NOODLE DISH

**KATHLEEN WHITSETT
GREENWOOD, IN**

Comfort in a skillet! This is a variation on a recipe from my grandmother and my mother, who are both wonderful cooks. I love the tastes and textures of this recipe and the shredded carrots give it a pop of color. Serve family-style in a large bowl with slices of buttered warm French bread.

16 to 24-oz. pkg. wide
  egg noodles, uncooked
8 slices bacon, diced
2 T. butter , sliced
1 T. olive oil
1 onion, chopped
1 c. carrot, peeled and
  shredded
1 head cabbage,
  shredded
1 clove garlic, minced
2 c. cooked ham, diced
salt and pepper to taste

Cook egg noodles according to package directions; drain. Meanwhile, in a large skillet over medium heat, cook bacon until crisp. Remove bacon to a paper towel, reserving one tablespoon drippings in skillet. Add butter and olive oil to drippings; stir. Add onion; cook until onion begins to soften, stirring often. Add carrot; cook until carrot begins to soften, stirring often. Add cabbage; cook until cabbage begins to soften, stirring often. Add garlic; cook and stir for one minute. Add ham and bacon; reduce heat to low. Simmer for a few minutes, until heated through. Add cooked noodles and stir gently. Season with salt and pepper.

Makes 4 to 6 servings.

JUDY'S SKILLET SPAGHETTI

**JUDY SCHROFF
CHURUBUSCO, IN**

This was one of my favorite go-to recipes while I was working and raising a family. It's very simple and uses ingredients most of us have in our pantries.

In a large skillet, brown beef over medium heat; drain. Add remaining ingredients except spaghetti and cheese. Cover and bring to a boil. Reduce heat to low. Simmer for 30 minutes, stirring occasionally. Add uncooked spaghetti and stir to separate strands. Cover and simmer another 30 minutes, stirring occasionally, or until spaghetti is tender. Serve sprinkled with grated Parmesan cheese.

Makes 6 servings.

1 lb. ground beef
3 c. water
2-1/4 c. tomato juice
6-oz. can tomato paste
2 T. dried, minced onion
2 T. chili powder
1 t. sugar
1 t. garlic salt
1 t. dried oregano
8-oz. pkg. spaghetti, uncooked
Garnish: grated Parmesan cheese

MOM'S BBQ CHICKEN

RONDA BRANNEMAN
JEFFERSONVILLE, IN

This is the best sauce...not too spicy like some! Everyone will love it...and no need to light the grill.

1 c. catsup
2 T. vinegar
2 T. onion, finely chopped
1 T. brown sugar, packed
1 T. Worcestershire sauce
1 t. sugar
1 t. paprika
1/4 t. salt
pepper to taste
2 to 3 lbs. chicken drumsticks or leg quarters
1/4 c. butter, melted

Combine all ingredients except chicken and butter in a microwave-safe one-quart bowl; mix well. Microwave, uncovered, on high setting for 5 minutes. Stir after 3 minutes, or when sauce is hot and thick enough to coat a spoon. Arrange chicken in a microwave-safe glass baking pan. Brush chicken with butter; spoon sauce over chicken. Cover with microwave-safe plastic wrap. Microwave on high setting for 25 to 30 minutes, until chicken juices run clear when pierced. Let stand, covered, for 5 minutes before serving.

Makes 4 to 6 servings.

KITCHEN TIP

A pat of homemade garlic butter really adds flavor to warm bread or steamed vegetables. Blend equal parts of softened butter and olive oil, then stir in finely chopped garlic to taste...so easy!

ZUCCHINI-CRUST PIZZA

LORINDA HERRELL
CONNERSVILLE, IN

My neighbor Joni, who's a registered nurse, shared this recipe with me, as I am diabetic and also a gardener with tons of zucchini. It's a tasty low-carb recipe that's a terrific way to use up zucchini. I tweaked it a little to make it more my own. These crusts freeze very well too. Enjoy!

In a strainer, press zucchini to remove as much liquid as possible. Combine zucchini and remaining ingredients except garnish in a bowl; stir well. Spread in a parchment paper-lined 12" round pizza pan. Smooth out mixture to cover pan. Bake at 375 degrees for 35 minutes, or until set. Top with desired toppings; return to oven until heated through. Cut into wedges to serve.

Makes 6 servings.

2 c. zucchini, shredded and packed
2 eggs, beaten
1/3 c. whole-wheat flour
1/2 c. shredded mozzarella cheese
1/2 c. shredded pizza-blend cheese
1 T. olive oil
1 T. fresh basil, chopped
Garnish: favorite pizza toppings

SHRIMP & MUSHROOM FETTUCCINE

DANI SIMMERS
KENDALLVILLE, IN

An excellent dish for company because it's oh-so-good and a little different. Serve with a fresh green salad, a basket of warm Italian bread and a big shaker of shredded Parmesan cheese.

12-oz. pkg. garlic & herb fettuccine pasta, uncooked

2 T. olive oil

1 lb. cooked medium shrimp

1 lb. sliced mushrooms

2 T. garlic, minced

10-oz. pkg. fresh spinach, thinly sliced

2 c. tomato sauce

2 T. chicken soup base

Cook pasta according to package directions; drain. Meanwhile, heat olive oil in a large skillet over medium heat. Sauté shrimp, mushrooms, garlic and spinach for several minutes, until mushrooms are tender and spinach is wilted. Remove mixture to a bowl with a slotted spoon, reserving drippings in skillet. Add tomato sauce and soup base to drippings. Stir well and bring to a boil. Return shrimp mixture to skillet and heat through; add cooked pasta and toss together.

Makes 6 servings.

TOMATO-SOY PORK CHOPS

ELAINE MATHIS
MARION, IN

My "I hate pork" grandson loves these!

Combine flour and seasonings in a plastic zipping bag; add pork chops and shake to coat. Heat oil in a large skillet over medium heat; brown pork chops on both sides. Drain; transfer to a 5-quart slow cooker. Top with remaining ingredients. Cover and cook on low setting for 3 to 3-1/2 hours, until pork chops are tender.

Makes 6 servings.

1/4 c. all-purpose flour
1/4 t. garlic powder
1/4 t. pepper
6 boneless pork chops
1/4 c. oil
3 T. soy sauce
1/3 c. water
1 onion, thinly sliced
14-1/2 oz. can diced
   tomatoes, drained

ITALIAN PEPPERONI PANINI

ANGELA DAVIS
GUILFORD, IN

One day, my husband took some leftovers and made an excellent sandwich. This recipe is my attempt to recreate the sandwich.

Sprinkle one bread slice with Parmesan cheese. Add pepperoni and ham; sprinkle with mozzarella cheese and top with remaining bread slice. Spread butter lightly over the outside of sandwich. Place on a countertop or panini grill; cook on high setting until golden and cheese is melted.

Makes one sandwich.

2 thin slices French
   bread
1 T. shredded Parmesan
   cheese
5 slices pepperoni
2 slices deli baked ham
2 T. shredded
   mozzarella cheese
softened butter to taste

CHEESY MACARONI BEEF

SHERRY PRESCOTT
WINCHESTER, IN

An easy supper dish! I first tried this recipe in a high school cooking class, 40 years ago. It's been a favorite since then because it's so easy to put together at the last minute, with items most everyone has on hand.

1/4 c. butter, sliced

2 c. elbow macaroni, uncooked

4 c. tomato juice

1 lb. lean ground beef

1 onion, chopped

1 t. salt

1/2 t. pepper

4 to 6 slices pasteurized process cheese

Melt butter in an electric skillet. Add uncooked macaroni; stir until coated. Add tomato juice and bring to a rapid boil. Add uncooked beef in small chunks, onion, salt and pepper. Cover and cook at 250 degrees for 20 minutes, or until beef is cooked and macaroni is tender. Uncover and stir. Arrange cheese slices on top; cover and cook just until cheese is melted.

Makes 4 servings.

DINNERTIME CONVERSATION

Indiana limestone is called Bedford limestone or Salem limestone. It is quarried in south central Indiana. Bedford limestone is the highest quality quarried limestone in the U.S.

BACON-WRAPPED BBQ CHICKEN

NICOLE CULVER
LA FONTAINE, IN

Over the 4th of July, my sister-in-law Kim cooked this chicken for us on her tiny grill, and I fell in love! Since then, my husband has added his own touch to it. Serve with corn on the cob, watermelon and a cold glass of iced tea for a sunny summer dinner.

In a saucepan over low heat, combine sauce, brown sugar and onion powder. Simmer for 30 minutes, stirring occasionally. Meanwhile, wrap chicken breasts with one to 2 slices bacon each; secure with wooden toothpicks. Set aside 3/4 cup of sauce mixture. Brush remaining sauce mixture over chicken. Place chicken on an oiled grate over medium-high heat. Grill for 30 minutes, turning occasionally, until nearly done. Brush chicken well with reserved sauce mixture. Cook until chicken juices run clear and sauce is caramelized.

18-oz. bottle favorite barbecue sauce, divided

2 T. brown sugar, packed

onion powder to taste

4 to 6 boneless, skinless chicken breasts

1/2 to 1 lb. bacon

Serves 4 to 6.

SPICY RUBBED PORK TENDERLOIN

LYNN RUSK
SOUTH BEND, IN

This recipe was given to me by my mother-in-law Lynette. It's a great go-to recipe for company or a busy day at home.

1 to 3 T. chili powder, to taste
1 t. salt
1 t. pepper
1/4 t. ground ginger
1/4 t. dried thyme
1/4 t. dry mustard
1-lb. pork tenderloin fillet

Mix together all spices in a bowl. Rub desired amount of spice mixture over both sides of tenderloin. Wrap tightly in aluminum foil; refrigerate for 8 hours to overnight. Unwrap tenderloin and place on an oiled grate over medium-high heat. Grill to desired doneness, turning once or twice, about 15 to 20 minutes. Remove tenderloin to a platter; let stand for 10 minutes. Slice thinly and serve with natural juices.

Makes 8 servings.

HAWAIIAN CHICKEN KABOBS

EMILY HARTZELL
PORTLAND, IN

Light the tiki torches! This is the perfect recipe for grilling out with family & friends on a balmy summer night.

In a small saucepan, stir together reserved pineapple juice, soy sauce, oil, brown sugar and seasonings. Bring to a boil over medium heat; reduce heat and simmer for 5 minutes. Cool slightly. Place chicken in a large shallow glass dish. Pour marinade over chicken; cover and chill for at least one hour. Drain, pouring marinade into a small saucepan; bring to a boil for 3 minutes. Wrap each chicken cube in a piece of bacon. Thread ingredients onto skewers, alternating chicken, pineapple and vegetables. Grill skewers over medium heat for 10 to 15 minutes, brushing often with marinade, until chicken juices run clear. Serve skewers over cooked rice.

Makes 6 servings.

15-1/4 oz. can pineapple chunks in juice, drained and 1/2 c. juice reserved

1/2 c. soy sauce

1/4 c. canola oil

1 T. brown sugar, packed

2 t. ground ginger

1 t. garlic powder

1 t. dry mustard

1/4 t. pepper

1-1/2 lbs. boneless, skinless chicken breasts, cut into 1-inch cubes

1 lb. bacon, cut into thirds

1 green pepper, cut into 1-inch squares

12 mushrooms

18 cherry tomatoes

6 skewers

cooked rice

CHAPTER FIVE

NOTRE DAME

Appetizers & Snacks

**WHETHER YOU ARE HAVING
COMPANY OR JUST NEED A
LITTLE SNACK TO HOLD YOU OVER
UNTIL THE NEXT MEAL, YOU'LL
FIND THESE RECIPES ARE GREAT
FOR TAKING ON-THE-GO OR AS A
FAVORITE APPETIZER.**

GOOD-FOR-YOU SNACK

MICKEY SCHEIVE
HIGHLAND, IN

Makes an ideal snack for the kids to munch on between classes.

6 c. doughnut-shaped
   oat cereal
1 c. salted peanuts
1 c. raisins
1 c. brown sugar, packed
1/2 c. butter, softened
1/4 c. corn syrup
1/2 t. salt
1/2 t. baking soda

Combine cereal, peanuts and raisins in a buttered large mixing bowl; set aside. Cook brown sugar, butter, corn syrup and salt in a saucepan over medium heat, stirring constantly until bubbly around the edges. Boil for 2 minutes, stirring occasionally. Remove from heat; stir in baking soda. Pour over cereal mixture; stir until well coated. Divide and spread evenly into 2 greased 13"x9" baking pans. Bake at 250 degrees for 15 minutes. Stir; let cool for 10 minutes. Loosen sides with a spatula; cool until firm, about 30 minutes. Break into bite-size pieces; store in an airtight container.

Makes about 20 servings.

BAJA BITES

PAM LEWIS
MUNSTER, IN

Nice 'n spicy tidbits that are oh-so easy to whip up!

5 eggs, beaten
1 c. cottage cheese
1/4 c. all-purpose flour
1/2 t. baking powder
1/4 c. butter, melted
2 T. green onion,
   minced
4-oz. can diced green
   chiles, drained

Combine eggs and cottage cheese; mix until almost smooth. Add flour, baking powder and butter; stir in onion, chiles and cheese. Pour into a lightly greased 8"x8" baking pan. Bake at 350 degrees for 30 to 40 minutes. Cool slightly; cut into squares.

Makes 9 servings.

STUFFED CUKE SNACKS

CAROLYN DECKARD
BEDFORD, IN

In summertime I raise cucumbers in my garden. Cucumbers are one of my favorite vegetables, so I love this recipe. This is good for any kind of showers or get-togethers. I make them to refrigerate to snack on, they are so good.

Run the tines of a fork lengthwise down cucumber on all sides. Trim both ends of cucumber; cut in half lengthwise. Use a spoon to remove and discard seeds. Place cucumber halves cut-side down on a paper towel to drain for 10 minutes. In a small bowl, blend cheeses, parsley, dill and onion; spoon into cucumber halves. Put halves back together; wrap in plastic wrap. Refrigerate for 3 to 4 hours. Cut into 1/2-inch slices; garnish with pimentos and dill.

Makes about 1-1/2 dozen.

1 cucumber

3-oz. pkg. cream cheese, softened

1 T. crumbled blue cheese

2 t. fresh parsley, chopped

2 t. fresh dill, minced

1 t. onion, grated

Garnish: sliced pimentos, additional fresh dill sprigs

PRESENTATION

When preparing appetizer trays, consider adding colorful fruits, fresh sprigs of mint and fresh flowers both on the platters and in small vases to make pretty garnishes.

ARTICHOKE & PARMESAN DIP

ANGELA DAVIS
GUILFORD, IN

This recipe is so easy and oh-so good! It is awesome for parties and get-togethers.

14-oz. can artichoke hearts, drained and chopped
1 c. mayonnaise
1 c. shredded Parmesan cheese
1 c. shredded mozzarella cheese
2 T. green onions, chopped
1/8 t. dried parsley
1/8 t. salt

Combine all ingredients in a bowl. Mix well; transfer to a greased 13"x9" baking pan. Bake, uncovered, at 350 degrees for 30 minutes, or until hot and bubbly.

Serves 6 to 8.

MINI COCKTAIL PIZZAS

CAROLYN DECKARD
BEDFORD, IN

These little treats are great for any party. I got this recipe years ago from my favorite aunt.

1 lb. ground pork sausage
2 5-oz. jars sharp pasteurized process cheese spread
1/4 c. catsup
3 T. Worcestershire sauce
1/4 t. dried oregano
2 16-oz. loaves party rye bread

Brown sausage in a skillet over medium heat; drain. Add remaining ingredients except bread; cook and stir over medium-low heat until mixed well. Remove from heat. Spread each slice of bread with 2 to 3 teaspoons sausage mixture. Arrange on aluminum foil-lined baking sheets. Bake at 400 degrees for 10 minutes, or until hot and bubbly.

Serves 8 to 10.

SWEET & SPICY GOODNESS APPETIZER DIP

KIMTOYIA SAM
INDIANAPOLIS, IN

My aunt was a wonderful hostess. Everyone's holiday parties started with her Sweet & Spicy Dip and crackers. It only takes a few minutes to make and it's delicious!

In a bowl, whisk together preserves, mustard, 2 tablespoons horseradish and pepper. Add more horseradish, if desired. Cover and chill. To serve, unwrap cream cheese and place on a serving plate; spoon preserves mixture over cream cheese. Serve with crackers.

Serves 8 to 10.

8-oz jar peach or apricot preserves
1 T. Dijon mustard
2 to 3 T. grated horseradish
cracked pepper to taste
8-oz. pkg. cream cheese, softened
buttery round crackers or chips

WARM PIZZA FONDUE

BETH FLACK
TERRE HAUTE, IN

This fondue is easy to make and stays warm in the slow cooker for serving. It's a favorite of family & friends, especially on Christmas Eve.

Combine all ingredients except crackers or bread sticks in a 3-quart slow cooker. Cover and cook on low setting for 2 hours, stirring often. Turn slow cooker to warm; serve with crackers or bread sticks.

Makes 30 servings.

2 10-3/4 oz. cans fiesta nacho cheese soup
6-oz. pkg. shredded pizza-blend cheese
3/4 c. pizza sauce
1/2 c. milk
1/2 c. pepperoni, chopped, or mini pepperoni slices
1 t. Italian seasoning
thin wheat crackers or crunchy bread sticks

CRABBY ARTICHOKE SPREAD

**KATHY GRASHOFF
FORT WAYNE, IN**

Your guests will just love this creamy, spicy dip!

1 jalapeño pepper, seeded and chopped

1 t. oil

14-oz. can artichokes, drained and chopped

2 6-oz. cans crabmeat, drained

1 c. mayonnaise

1/2 red pepper, chopped

1/2 c. grated Parmesan cheese

2 green onions, chopped

2 t. lemon juice

2 t. Worcestershire sauce

1/2 t. celery seed

toasted bread rounds or crackers

Sauté jalapeño in oil until tender. Combine jalapeño and remaining ingredients except bread rounds or crackers in a slow cooker. Cover and cook on low setting for 4 hours. Serve with bread rounds or crackers.

Makes 3 to 4 cups.

FAMILY-TIME CONVERSATION

Indiana is the first state to have a chapel in its state capitol. It was built in memory of former first lady Beth Bowen.

PARMESAN PARTY LOG

CAROLYN DECKARD
BEDFORD, IN

This tasty recipe has been in our family for years. It's something different to serve at showers and other parties. A good make-ahead!

In a bowl, combine cream cheese, Parmesan cheese and salt; mix until well blended. Add green pepper and pimentos; mix well. Cover and chill. At serving time, form into a log shape; coat with chopped parsley. May be made a few days ahead and kept refrigerated.

Makes 8 servings.

8-oz. pkg. cream cheese, softened

1/2 c. grated Parmesan cheese

1/4 t. onion salt or garlic salt

2 T. green pepper, chopped

2 T. diced pimentos, drained

Garnish: chopped fresh parsley

SWEET CHICKEN-BACON WRAPS

RENITA SECREST
JASONVILLE, IN

This recipe is shared in memory of my daughter's mother-in-law, Theresa Chambers. She gave it to me over ten years ago. She was a great cook. We make these for holidays and football games.

Wrap each chicken cube in a piece of bacon. Secure with wooden toothpicks; set aside. Combine brown sugar and chili powder; coat chicken cubes well and place into plastic zipping bags. Refrigerate overnight to marinate. Place chicken cubes on a rimmed baking sheet coated with non-stick vegetable spray. Bake at 350 degrees for 30 to 45 minutes, until bacon is crisp and chicken juices run clear when pierced.

Serves 6 to 8.

4 boneless, skinless chicken breasts, cut into 1-inch cubes

1 c. brown sugar, packed

2 T. chili powder

1 lb. bacon, cut into thirds

LEMON-DILL SNACK MIX

KRISTA MARSHALL
FORT WAYNE, IN

My mom used to make this tasty snack mix when I was little, and now I make it for my family. Bet you can't eat just one bite!

2 12-oz. pkgs. oyster crackers
1 c. canola oil
2 1-oz. pkgs. ranch salad dressing mix
2 t. dried dill weed
1 t. garlic powder
1/2 t. lemon pepper

Spread crackers in a large roasting pan; set aside. In a bowl, stir together oil and seasonings. Pour over crackers and stir gently. Bake, uncovered, at 350 degrees for 30 minutes, stirring every 10 minutes. Turn off oven; leave pan in oven until cooled.

Makes 10 servings.

GRANDMA'S HOT SAUSAGE BALLS

BETH FLACK
TERRE HAUTE, IN

A family favorite...everyone loves these for parties or even brunch.

1 lb. hot ground pork sausage
5-oz. jar sharp pasteurized process cheese spread
3 c. biscuit baking mix
1/4 c. whole milk

Combine all ingredients in a large bowl. Mix well; roll into bite-size balls and place on a baking sheet. Freeze for 3 hours, or until firm. When ready to serve, bake at 400 degrees for 20 minutes, or until hot and golden.

Makes 3 dozen.

BRAUNSCHWEIGER SPREAD

**BARBARA KLEIN
NEWBURGH, IN**

I love to make this hearty spread for holiday parties. Serve with regular or buttery whole-wheat crackers or shredded wheat crackers. Guests will love it!

In a large bowl, mash braunschweiger with a fork. Add half of cream cheese, pickle juice, sauces and garlic salt. Beat thoroughly with an electric mixer on medium speed until blended. Mix in butter, onion and pickles. Pack mixture into an aluminum foil-lined bowl; cover and refrigerate for 2 hours. To serve, turn out on a plate; remove foil. Spread remaining cream cheese over ball and coat with pecans.

Serves 10.

8-oz. pkg. braunschweiger

8-oz. pkg. cream cheese, softened and divided

2 t. dill pickle juice

1 t. Worcestershire sauce

3 drops hot pepper sauce

1/4 t. garlic salt

1/4 c. butter, softened

1/4 c. onion, chopped

1/3 c. dill pickle chips, drained and chopped

1/2 c. chopped pecans

KITCHEN TIP

A jar of dried, minced onion can be a real timesaver! If the recipe has a lot of liquid, such as soups and stews, it's easy to switch. Just substitute one tablespoon of dried, minced onion for every 1/3 cup fresh diced onion.

BEST DEVILED EGGS

ESTHER BAIR
CHURUBUSCO, IN

Great-Grandma always garnished her deviled eggs with a dash of paprika and a slice of olive.

6 to 8 eggs
2 T. mayonnaise, or more to taste
1/2 t. mustard
2 t. sugar
1 t. vinegar

Place eggs in a large saucepan; cover generously with water. Bring to a low boil over high heat. Reduce heat to a simmer; simmer for 18 minutes. Drain water from pan. Cover eggs with cold water, shaking pan to crack eggshells. Drain; repeat 2 to 3 times. Peel eggs; cut in half lengthwise and remove yolks. Mash yolks with a fork, breaking up any chunks. Mix all ingredients into yolks until smooth and well combined, adding more mayonnaise if a creamier consistency is desired. Spoon filling into egg whites. Chill.

Makes 12 to 16.

CHUNKY SALSA DIP

CHRISTI VAWTER
SHERIDAN, IN

Wherever I take this dip, it's the star of the show! I always end up sharing the recipe, which was passed to me by my sixth-grade teacher, Mrs. Weaver. It's also tasty spooned onto tacos, burgers and grilled chicken.

1 lb. mild Cheddar cheese, coarsely shredded
2 avocados, peeled, pitted and diced
12 roma tomatoes, diced
2 bunches green onions, diced
32-oz. jar salsa verde
tortilla chips

Add cheese and vegetables to a very large bowl; do not stir. Cover and refrigerate until ready to serve. At serving time, pour salsa over all. Stir very gently, just enough to combine ingredients. Serve with tortilla chips.

Makes 24 servings.

PORK & APPLE BITES

LYNN WILLIAMS
MUNCIE, IN

We love party meatballs, but I was looking for something a little different. These are perfect for a fall tailgating party!

In a large bowl; combine pork and seasonings; mix well. Add apple, bread crumbs and walnuts; mix gently until well blended. Form mixture into balls by tablespoonfuls. Working in batches, brown meatballs in a large skillet over medium heat. Drain; return all meatballs to skillet. Pour water into skillet; cover tightly. Cook over medium-low heat for 15 minutes, or until meatballs are no longer pink in the center. Remove meatballs to a serving bowl; cover and set aside. Stir apple jelly into drippings in skillet; cook and stir until jelly is melted. Spoon sauce over meatballs.

Makes about 3 dozen.

1 lb. ground pork
1/4 t. cinnamon
1 t. salt
1/8 t. pepper
1/2 c. Granny Smith apple, peeled, cored and grated
1/4 c. soft rye bread crumbs
1/4 c. chopped walnuts
1/2 c. water
1/2 c. apple jelly

JUST FOR FUN

One of the biggest mysteries ever in Indiana was where the name "Hoosier" ever came from. This explanation came close, when a Quaker from Richmond, Virginia, by the name of Sarah Harvey wrote in an 1835 letter about the "old settlers in Indiana...called 'Hooshers.'" She explained that a 'Hoosher' was actually a type of cabin called a 'Hoosher nest,' and that's what those settlers lived in. That sounds pretty accurate, but still to this day, people debate about the nickname of every Indiana resident.

BLENDER HUMMUS

KATHY GRASHOFF
FORT WAYNE, IN

This is quick for drop-ins! Take it out on your deck and enjoy.

15-oz. can garbanzo
  beans, drained
juice of 4 lemons
3 cloves garlic, pressed
1 t. Asian sesame oil
salt to taste
pita chips, cut-up
  vegetables

In a blender, combine all ingredients except chips and vegetables. Cover and process until smooth. If too thick, add a little water, one to 2 teaspoons at a time, until desired consistency. Transfer to a bowl; cover and refrigerate. Serve with pita chips and vegetables.

Makes about 1-1/2 cups.

PUDDIE'S PEEL & EAT SHRIMP

CRIS GOODE
MOORESVILLE, IN

My husband makes this tasty treat for my extended family over a campfire when we visit Memaw and Papaw at horse camp!

1 T. seasoned salt
1 T. seafood seasoning
1 T. chili powder
1 t. canola oil
12-oz. pkg. frozen
  uncooked jumbo
  shrimp, thawed and
  cleaned

In a large bowl, mix seasonings and oil. Add shrimp and toss to coat; let stand for 20 minutes. Drain, discarding marinade. Place shrimp on a grill over medium-high heat. Cook for 5 to 10 minutes, until shrimp are pink. Peel and eat.

Serves 4 to 6.

PUB BEER DIP

KAREN HAZELETT
FREMONT, IN

We enjoy the time we spend at Lake James in northeast Indiana. Winters at the lake are lonely for year 'rounders, so we started a monthly card club with five other couples. It's a terriffic way to see your neighbors during colder months and try each other's recipes. Our friend Jan is a wonderful hostess and shared this slow-cooker recipe with us. It was an immediate hit!

In a 2-1/2 to 3-quart slow cooker, mix together cheeses, beer and sauces. Cover and cook on low setting for 2 hours, stirring occasionally. Dip will become thicker the longer it cooks. Stir in bacon just before serving. Serve with pretzels, crackers or bread.

Makes about 4 cups.

2 5-oz. jars sharp Cheddar cheese spread

8-oz. pkg. cream cheese, softened

1/2 c. regular or non-alcoholic beer

1 t. Worcestershire sauce

5 to 6 drops hot pepper sauce

4 to 5 slices bacon, crisply cooked and crumbled

pretzels, crackers, bread slices

HOT SAUSAGE DIP

LAURA AIVAZ
PLAINVILLE, IN

When my sister-in-law and I first tried this dip, we could not stop eating it! It has become a family favorite for any kind of party.

Brown sausage in a large skillet over medium heat; drain. Add tomatoes; heat through. Add cream cheese; simmer until melted and stir well. Keep warm in skillet over low heat. Serve with corn or tortilla chips.

Serves 12.

16-oz. pkg. hot or mild ground pork sausage

15-oz. can diced tomatoes with green chiles, drained

2 8-oz. pkgs. cream cheese, softened

corn or tortilla chips

HOT BACON & SWISS DIP

MARLA CALDWELL
FOREST, IN

Always a favorite...the flavor combination is unbeatable.

8-oz. pkg. cream cheese, softened
1/2 c. mayonnaise
1 c. shredded Swiss cheese
2 T. green onion, chopped
8 slices bacon, crisply cooked and crumbled, divided
1/2 c. buttery round crackers, crushed

Combine cream cheese, mayonnaise, Swiss cheese and onion. Mix well; blend in half of the bacon. Spread in a small baking dish; top with remaining bacon and crushed crackers. Bake at 350 degrees for 15 minutes. Serve warm.

Makes about 3 cups.

MINI PARMESAN CORN COBS

KRISTA MARSHALL
FORT WAYNE, IN

We love our summer pool parties, and it's always fun to plan the food. Mini ears of corn are much easier to handle!

3 ears corn, husked and broken in half
1/4 c. grated Parmesan cheese
4 t. dried parsley salt to taste
6 T. butter, melted

Bring a large pot of water to a boil over high heat. Add corn and cook until tender, about 6 minutes. Drain well. Combine cheese, parsley and salt in a cup; mix well. Use a pastry brush to coat hot corn with butter; sprinkle with cheese mixture. Let stand about one minute before serving, so cheese mixture sticks.

Makes 6 servings.

ITALIAN MEATBALLS

SHARI MILLER
HOBART, IN

So versatile...these can be served as an appetizer, over pasta or rice, or even make great sub sandwiches.

Combine ground beef, bread crumbs, milk, onion, garlic salt and pepper in a bowl just until mixed. Shape into 48 small meatballs; set aside. Cut cheese into 48, 1/2-inch cubes. Push a cheese cube into the center of each meatball, covering the cheese completely. Roll meatballs lightly in flour. Heat oil in a large skillet and cook meatballs just until browned; drain. Add pizza sauce to skillet. Bring to a boil over medium heat; reduce heat, cover and simmer for 25 to 30 minutes, or until meatballs are no longer pink.

Makes 4 dozen.

2 lbs. ground beef
2 c. seasoned dry bread crumbs
1 c. milk
1/4 c. dried, minced onion
2 t. garlic salt
1/4 t. pepper
8-oz. pkg. mozzarella cheese
1/3 c. all-purpose flour
1/4 c. oil
4 15-oz. jars pizza sauce

TNT DIP

TERESA STIEGELMEYER
INDIANAPOLIS, IN

Make this peppery slow-cooker dip even spicer by adding hot pepper sauce to taste or using extra-hot salsa...if you dare!

In a large saucepan over medium heat, combine all ingredients except chips and bread. Cook and stir until bubbly and cheese is melted. If preferred, combine all ingredients except chips and bread in a slow cooker. Cover and cook on high setting for about one hour, stirring occasionally. Serve with corn chips or party rye bread.

Serves 10 to 12.

1-1/2 lbs. ground beef, browned and drained
10-3/4 oz. can cream of mushroom soup
1 c. salsa
1/4 c. butter, melted
2 T. chili powder
16-oz. pkg. pasteurized process cheese spread, cubed
corn chips, party rye bread

ROASTED GARLIC SPREAD

MARGARET CALLAM
GEORGETOWN, IN

This is a delicious appetizer. It's not only a family favorite, but a crowd-pleaser as well. The garlic mellows as it cooks. Great for a holiday gathering, football tailgate or a company potluck.

4 whole heads garlic

1/4 c. extra-virgin olive oil

2 8-oz. pkgs. cream cheese, softened

1/2 c. butter, softened

1 t. salt

1/4 c. fresh chives, minced

sliced French bread, warmed

Cut the tops off garlic heads, leaving heads intact. Arrange heads in a small casserole dish; drizzle with olive oil. Cover with aluminum foil. Bake at 350 degrees for 45 minutes. Uncover and bake an additional 10 minutes, or until garlic is soft. Remove from oven; cool completely. When garlic heads are cool, remove and discard outermost layers of the papery skin. Scoop out soft garlic pulp with a small spoon and set aside. Beat cream cheese and butter with an electric mixer on high speed until light and fluffy. Add garlic pulp and salt; beat again until blended. Stir in chives. Serve spread over warm slices of French bread. May keep refrigerated up to 2 weeks.

Makes 2-1/2 cups.

MIMI'S LITTLE BARBECUE SAUSAGES

BEVERLY ELKINS
BLOOMINGTON, IN

These sausages are so easy and delicious...a great finger food for football games. My grandchildren call me "Mimi." The first time my youngest grandchild ate these little sausages, he asked me, "Are these Mimi's sausages?" I said, "Yes, they are!" and the name stuck. They are a favorite of all my family and they are requested at all our family get-togethers.

Arrange sausages in a 13"x9" baking pan sprayed with non-stick vegetable spray; set aside. Combine remaining ingredients in a microwave-safe dish. Microwave on high for 2 minutes; stir, then microwave for one more minute. Spoon mixture over sausages. Bake, uncovered, at 350 degrees for 15 to 20 minutes.

14-oz. pkg. mini smoked beef sausages
1/2 c. catsup
1 T. Worcestershire sauce
1 c. brown sugar, packed

Serves 6 to 8.

EASY GUACAMOLE

KRISTA MARSHALL
FORT WAYNE, IN

Guacamole is one of my favorite dips...I can even make a meal out of it! So this easy version is great for a quick lunch. Serve with tortilla chips or your favorite snack crackers.

Place avocados in a bowl; mash to desired consistency using a potato masher or a fork. Add remaining ingredients; mix all together. For the best flavor, cover and chill for one hour before serving.

2 avocados, peeled, pitted and chopped
1/4 tomato, chopped
2 T. onion, chopped
2 T. olive oil
juice of 1/2 lemon
1/2 t. kosher salt
pepper to taste

Serves 4 to 6.

CHAPTER SIX

DEAR SANTA

Desserts

THERE IS ALWAYS ROOM FOR
DESSERT. SO WHEN YOUR SWEET
TOOTH IS CALLING, THESE SIMPLE
SWEETS ARE THE PERFECT WAY TO
END THE DAY...SANTA WILL LOVE
THEM TOO!

CREAM CHEESE-FILLED CUPCAKES

MELISSA MISHLER
COLUMBIA CITY, IN

These are so delicious, you might want to make a double batch!

18-1/4 oz. pkg. German chocolate cake mix
1 c. mini semi-sweet chocolate chips
1/3 c. sugar
1 egg, beaten
8-oz. pkg. cream cheese, softened

Prepare cake mix according to package directions. Fill paper-lined muffin cups 1/2 full. Combine remaining ingredients; drop by teaspoonfuls onto batter. Bake at 350 degrees for 20 to 25 minutes. Cool completely.

Makes about 2 dozen.

MILK CHOCOLATE BROWNIES

CAROLYN GOCHENAUR
HOWE, IN

My sister-in-law gave me this recipe and it's been a favorite for many years.

1/2 c. butter, melted
2 c. plus 2 T. sugar, divided
4 eggs, beaten
2 t. vanilla extract
1-1/2 c. all-purpose flour
1/2 c. baking cocoa
1/2 t. salt
1 c. flaked coconut
1/2 c. milk chocolate chips
1/2 c. chopped pecans

In a large bowl, mix together melted butter and 2 cups sugar. Add eggs and vanilla; stir until well mixed and set aside. In another bowl, sift together flour, baking cocoa and salt; add to butter mixture and stir well. Add coconut and stir until just mixed. Pour batter into a greased and floured 13"x9" baking pan; sprinkle with chocolate chips, pecans and remaining sugar. Bake at 350 degrees for 25 minutes, or until a toothpick comes out clean. Cool; cut into squares.

Makes 15 brownies.

RASPBERRY CUSTARD PIE

SARAH SWANSON
NOBLESVILLE, IN

*Our five-year-old daughter collected raspberries every day for a week and
wanted to bake a pie. So we made this pie...she & our other kids loved it!*

Whisk together eggs and sour cream in a large bowl;
set aside. In a separate bowl, combine raspberries,
sugar, flour and salt; toss lightly. Add berry mixture to
sour cream mixture; mix well and pour into unbaked
crust. Bake at 350 degrees for 45 minutes, until firm
and golden. Cool completely.

Serves 6 to 8.

2 eggs, beaten
8-oz. container sour
  cream
1-1/2 to 2 c. fresh
  raspberries
1 c. sugar
1 T. all-purpose flour
1/2 t. salt
9-inch pie crust,
  unbaked

NOODLE KUGEL

GAIL FLUSCHE-HILL
HAMMOND, IN

*My whole family loves this sweet dish... it's always a hit every
holiday!*

Cook noodles according to package directions;
drain. Combine noodles and remaining ingredients
in a greased 13"x9" baking pan. Bake, uncovered,
at 350 degrees for one hour, or until heated through.
Top with cinnamon, if using.

Serves 10-12.

16-oz. pkg. wide egg
  noodles, uncooked
3/4 to 1 c. butter, melted
16-oz. container sour
  cream
20-oz. can crushed
  pineapple, drained
4 eggs, beaten
1 c. sugar
1/2 t. salt
2 t. vanilla extract
Optional: cinnamon

RED VELVET CAKE

**PEGGY FRAZIER
INDIANAPOLIS, IN**

When my daughter Julie was young, I helped her make this cake for a fundraiser. She won first prize and still has the blue ribbon!

2-1/2 c. all-purpose flour
1-1/2 c. sugar
1 t. salt
1 t. baking cocoa
1 c. buttermilk
1-1/2 c. oil
2 eggs, beaten
1 t. vanilla extract
1-oz. bottle red food coloring
1 t. white vinegar
1 t. baking soda

In a large bowl, mix flour, sugar, salt and cocoa. Add buttermilk, oil, eggs and vanilla; mix well. Stir in food coloring. Mix vinegar and baking soda; add to batter and stir just until well blended. Pour into 3 greased and floured 9" round cake pans. Bake at 325 degrees for 30 to 35 minutes, until a toothpick tests clean. Cool; assemble with frosting.

Cream Cheese Frosting:
Blend cream cheese, butter and vanilla. Stir in powdered sugar until smooth; add nuts, if using.

Serves 10 to 12.

CREAM CHEESE FROSTING

8-oz. pkg. cream cheese, softened
1/2 c. butter, softened
1 t. vanilla extract
6 c. powdered sugar
Optional: chopped pecans

CHOCOLATE & MARSHMALLOW CUPCAKES

KATHY GRASHOFF
FORT WAYNE, IN

Drizzle with chocolate or caramel sauce for a divine delight!

Place chocolate and butter together in a microwave-safe bowl; microwave on high setting just until melted. Cool slightly, just until warm. Blend together eggs and sugar until light and foamy. Add flour and salt; mix well. Pour in chocolate mixture; blend until smooth. Fill paper-lined muffin cups 2/3 full. Sprinkle one teaspoon chocolate chips over each cupcake. Bake at 350 degrees for 15 minutes, until a toothpick tests clean. Remove from oven; arrange several marshmallows on top of each cupcake. Broil just until marshmallows turn golden. Remove from oven and let stand 5 minutes to cool slightly.

Makes one dozen.

8-oz. pkg. unsweetened dark baking chocolate, chopped

1 c. butter, softened

4 eggs

1 c. sugar

3/4 c. all-purpose flour

1 t. salt

1/2 c. mini semi-sweet chocolate chips

Garnish: 1/2 c. mini marshmallows

PRESENTATION

You're never too old for party favors! Send your guests home with a whimsical memento...tiny potted plants, little bags of homemade candy, mini photo frames or even bottles of bubbles.

MARBLE CHEESECAKE

SHARON DENNISON
FLOYDS KNOBS, IN

I've been making this cheesecake for years. My family really loves when I bring it to gatherings.

1 c. graham cracker
   crumbs
3 T. sugar
3 T. margarine, melted
3 8-oz. pkgs. cream
   cheese, softened
3/4 c. sugar
3 T. all-purpose flour
1 t. vanilla extract
3 eggs, beaten
1-oz. sq. unsweetened
   baking chocolate,
   melted and cooled
   slightly

In a bowl, combine cracker crumbs, sugar and margarine; press into the bottom of a 9" springform pan. Bake at 350 degrees for 10 minutes. With an electric mixer on medium speed, beat cream cheese, sugar, flour and vanilla until well blended. Blend in eggs. Remove one cup of batter to a separate bowl and blend in melted chocolate. Spoon plain and chocolate batters alternately over crust. Use a knife to swirl through batter several times for marble effect. Bake at 450 degrees for 10 minutes. Reduce oven to 250 degrees; bake an additional 30 minutes. Loosen pan's rim, but do not remove. Let cool; remove rim.

Serves 10.

FRENCH STRAWBERRIES

KATHY GRASHOFF
FORT WAYNE, IN

Sweet berries blended with a hint of cinnamon make this dessert extra-special.

4 c. strawberries, hulled
   and halved
3 T. frozen orange juice
   concentrate, thawed
1/2 c. plus 2 T. powdered
   sugar, divided
1 c. whipping cream
2 T. sour cream
1/8 t. vanilla extract
1/4 t. cinnamon

Sprinkle strawberries with orange juice concentrate and 1/2 cup sugar; gently stir. Refrigerate about 1-1/2 hours. In another mixing bowl, with an electric mixer on high speed, beat cream until soft peaks form; stir in remaining sugar, sour cream, vanilla and cinnamon. Gently fold chilled strawberries into whipped cream mixture.

Makes 4 to 6 servings.

STRAWBERRY DESSERT

JANICE NICHOLS
NORTH MANCHESTER, IN

A lady where I worked would surprise the department with this delicious dessert. The sight of those fresh, red strawberries would make your mouth water!

Slice cookie dough and press into the bottom of an ungreased 13"x9" baking pan. Bake at 350 degrees for 13 to 16 minutes, until lightly golden. Cool completely on a wire rack. Mix cream cheese and one cup whipped topping. Spread over cookie crust. Stir strawberries and glaze together and spread over top. Cover and chill. Cut into squares and serve with remaining whipped topping.

Serves 10 to 12.

16-1/2 oz. tube refrigerated sugar cookie dough

8-oz. pkg. cream cheese, softened

8-oz. container frozen whipped topping, thawed and divided

1 qt. strawberries, hulled and sliced

13-1/2 oz. container strawberry glaze

STRAWBERRY-RHUBARB PIE

SARAH PUTNAM
BOONVILLE, IN

I got this recipe from a friend and my whole family loves it...even my kids who are rather hesitant to try new things!

In a bowl, mix together one cup sugar and flour; set aside. Line a 9" pie plate with one unbaked crust. Spoon one cup strawberries and one cup rhubarb into crust. Sprinkle half of sugar mixture over fruit in crust. Repeat layers with remaining strawberries, rhubarb and sugar mixture; dot with butter. Cover with top crust; seal edges and cut 3 slits in the top to vent. Cover edge of crust with strips of aluminum foil. Bake at 425 degrees for 40 to 50 minutes, until golden, removing foil 15 minutes before pie is done.

Serves 8.

1 c. plus 1 T. sugar, divided

1/3 c. all-purpose flour

2 9-inch pie crusts

2 c. strawberries, hulled, sliced and divided

2 c. rhubarb, chopped and divided

2 T. butter, sliced

CRUMB-TOPPED RHUBARB

LAURA FULLER
FORT WAYNE, IN

Every summer, my sisters and I went to stay with my grandmother in her small-town home for a week. Every day she'd send us out to her garden to see how the rhubarb was coming along. Finally the time came, and she baked this delicious dessert for us. Such memories!

3 c. rhubarb, diced
1/2 c. sugar
7 T. all-purpose flour, divided
1 t. cinnamon
1/8 t. salt
1/2 c. brown sugar, packed
1/2 c. quick-cooking oats, uncooked
6 T. butter

In a large bowl, combine rhubarb, sugar, one tablespoon flour, cinnamon and salt. Mix well; spoon into a greased 12"x8" baking pan and set aside. In a separate bowl, combine remaining flour, brown sugar and oats. Cut in butter with a fork until crumbly; sprinkle over rhubarb mixture. Bake at 350 degrees for 40 minutes, or until bubbly and lightly golden.

Makes 8 servings.

MAPLE-BROWN SUGAR APPLE CRUMBLE

SHELLY SMITH
DANA, IN

The smell of this apple dessert in the oven really puts us in the mood for leaf raking, pumpkin carving and all our other favorite fall activities.

5 apples, peeled, cored and sliced
2/3 c. maple syrup
1/2 c. butter, softened
1/2 c. brown sugar, packed
3/4 c. all-purpose flour
3/4 c. long-cooking oats, uncooked
1/8 t. salt

Place sliced apples in a lightly greased 8"x8" baking pan; drizzle maple syrup over apples. In a bowl, blend together butter and brown sugar. Stir in flour, oats and salt until crumbly. Sprinkle butter mixture over apples. Bake, uncovered, at 375 degrees for 35 minutes, or until golden and apples are tender.

Serves 4.

SUPREME CARAMEL APPLE ROLLS

TRACEY GRAHAM
CHURUBUSCO, IN

This is one of my family's most-requested recipes. One time after serving them, one of my seven brothers told me, "These rolls are so bad, I need to take the rest home with me to eat!"

Combine pie filling and ice cream topping in a large bowl; pour into a greased 13"x9" baking pan. Sprinkle pecans, if using, over mixture. Combine cream cheese and powdered sugar in a bowl; set aside. Separate crescent roll dough into 2 rectangles; press perforations to seal. Spread half of cream cheese mixture over each rectangle. Starting with long side of each rectangle, roll up and seal edges. Cut each roll into 12 slices with a serrated knife. Stir together sugar and brown sugar in a bowl; dip slices in melted butter and then coat with sugar mixture. Arrange slices in baking pan. Bake at 400 degrees for 25 to 30 minutes, until center rolls are golden. Immediately invert onto a serving plate. Serve warm.

Makes 2 dozen rolls.

21-oz. can apple pie filling

1/2 c. caramel ice cream topping

Optional: 1/2 c. chopped pecans

8-oz. pkg. cream cheese, softened

1/3 c. powdered sugar

2 8-oz. tubes refrigerated crescent rolls

1/2 c. sugar

1/2 c. brown sugar, packed

1/2 c. butter, melted

GRAHAM CRACKER DELIGHT

PAM HOOLEY
LAGRANGE, IN

When I was young, we were happy without much prosperity. I didn't realize how poor we were until I grew up! My mom would make this for a special treat for us kids, and we thought it was as good as candy, which we rarely had the opportunity to eat.

16 double graham crackers, crushed

1 egg, beaten

1 c. brown sugar, packed

2 T. baking cocoa

1/2 c. butter, melted

1 t. vanilla extract

Optional: 1/2 c. chopped nuts

Place crushed crackers in a bowl; set aside. In a saucepan, beat together egg, brown sugar and cocoa; stir in melted butter. Cook over medium-low heat for several minutes, stirring constantly. Remove from heat; stir in vanilla and nuts, if using. Spoon mixture over crackers; mix well. Transfer to a greased 9"x9" baking pan; press well to compact it together. Let cool; cut into bars.

Makes 9 to 12 servings.

AUNT BESSIE'S FRESH APPLE CAKE

SHARON GOSS
INDIANAPOLIS, IN

My dad had five sisters who were all wonderful cooks. Each sister had a specialty. Cakes and desserts were my Aunt Bessie's specialty. Without a doubt, my favorite was her Fresh Apple Cake. It was like biting into an autumn day!

2 eggs, beaten

1 c. oil

2 c. sugar

1 t. vanilla extract

2-1/2 c. self-rising flour

1 T. cinnamon

3 c. apples, peeled, cored and diced

1 c. chopped walnuts

In a large bowl, beat eggs, oil and sugar with an electric mixer on medium speed. Mix in vanilla; set aside. In another bowl, sift together flour and cinnamon; add to egg mixture. Fold in apples and walnuts. Divide batter between 2 greased 8"x8" baking pans. Bake at 350 degrees for about 45 minutes. May also use a 13"x9" baking pan; bake for about one hour. Cut into squares.

Makes 18 servings.

SECRET-RECIPE
BIRTHDAY CAKE

SARA VOGES
WASHINGTON, IN

This is my super-secret, super-moist, better-than-a-bakery birthday cake. My kids love this fluffy icing too! Sometimes I will whip up some of the icing and just serve it with fruit...it's that good.

In a large bowl, stir together dry cake and pudding mixes, milk and eggs. Beat with an electric mixer on high speed for 2 minutes. Spread batter in a greased 13"x9" baking pan. Bake at 350 degrees for 20 minutes, or until a toothpick inserted in center tests done. Cool; top with Whipped Icing.

Whipped Icing:
In a bowl, whisk together dry pudding mix and milk until thickened. Fold in whipped topping. Cover and refrigerate for one to 2 hours before using.

Makes 1 to 18 servings.

16-1/2 oz. pkg. French
  vanilla cake mix
3.4-oz. pkg. French
  vanilla instant
  pudding mix
2 c. milk
2 eggs, beaten

WHIPPED ICING
3.4-oz pkg. French
  vanilla instant
  pudding mix
1 c. milk
8-oz. container frozen
  whipped topping,
  thawed

PRESENTATION

Wrap sandwiches for your garden party in wax paper and tie with a length of gingham ribbon. Serve them in a favorite basket lined with a vintage tea towel.

SHELLY'S STRAWBERRY TRIFLE

SHELLY SMITH
DANA, IN

A great summer dessert!

2 qts. fresh
strawberries, hulled
and sliced

3 T. sugar

3/4 t. almond extract,
divided

2 8-oz. pkgs. cream
cheese, softened

8-oz. container sour
cream

16-oz. container frozen
whipped topping,
thawed

2 c. powdered sugar

1/2 t. vanilla extract

16-oz. pkg. frozen angel
food cake, thawed

In a large bowl, toss strawberries with sugar and 1/4 teaspoon almond extract; set aside. In another large bowl, combine cream cheese, sour cream, whipped topping, powdered sugar, vanilla and remaining almond extract. Blend well; set aside. Tear cake into bite-sized pieces; fold into cream cheese mixture. In a large glass trifle dish, layer 1/3 each of cream cheese mixture and strawberry mixture. Repeat layering twice. Cover and chill until serving time.

Serves 12.

CHOCOLATE BURRITOS

JONI WALLMAN
INDIANAPOLIS, IN

A great recipe that can be made ahead for camping trips. Yummy with a scoop of ice cream and drizzled with chocolate sauce!

1 flour tortilla

1 to 2 T. chocolate chips

1 to 2 T. peanut butter

1 to 2 T. mini
marshmallows

Place tortilla on a piece of aluminum foil. Spread with a thin layer of peanut butter; sprinkle with chocolate chips and marshmallows. Fold in the end of the flour tortilla and roll up. Wrap folded tortilla in foil. Cook over a campfire or grill until ingredients are melted, or bake at 350 degrees for 10 to 12 minutes.

Serves one.

CHOCOLATE SILK PIE

**JAMIE MOFFATT
FRENCH LICK, IN**

Cut generous slices of this pie...everyone will love it!

Combine sugar, salt, cocoa and flour in a saucepan over medium heat. Slowly pour in milk, stirring constantly. Pour in egg yolks; stir well for 5 to 6 minutes. Remove saucepan from heat; stir in butter and vanilla. Pour mixture into pie crust. Refrigerate for 8 hours. Top with whipped topping and chocolate chips. Garnish with fresh mint leaves.

Serves 6 to 8.

1 c. sugar
1/8 t. salt
1/2 c. baking cocoa
1/2 c. all-purpose flour
2 c. milk
3 egg yolks
4 T. butter
1 t. vanilla extract
9-inch graham cracker pie crust
8-oz. container frozen whipped topping, thawed
1/2 c. chocolate chips
Garnish: mint leaves

JUST FOR FUN

A Christmas Story (1983) is set in Hammond, Indiana, the hometown of Jean Shepherd, the author who wrote the book on which the film was based,

DUTCH OVEN PEACH COBBLER

CHERYL PANNING
WABASH, IN

I've been making this dessert since I was a new bride over 40 years ago. It's very easy to do and the results are delicious!

29-oz. can sliced peaches, drained
1-1/2 c. sugar, divided
1 t. butter, melted
1 c. all-purpose flour
2 t. baking powder
1/2 t. salt
1/2 c. milk
1/2 c. water

Prepare a campfire with plenty of hot charcoal briquets. Place peaches in a greased 10" Dutch oven; set near fire to warm. In a bowl, mix 1/2 cup sugar and butter. In a separate bowl, mix flour, baking powder and salt. Stir flour mixture and milk into sugar mixture. Pour batter over peaches. Sprinkle with remaining sugar; pour water over batter without stirring. Arrange 7 hot charcoal briquets in a ring; set Dutch oven on top. Add lid; place 14 briquets on lid. Cook for about one hour, until bubbly and golden. Every 15 minutes, carefully rotate Dutch oven 1/4 turn to the right and rotate lid 1/4 turn to the left. Replace briquets on lid as needed. Cobbler may also be baked in a greased 10" round baking pan. Bake at 350 degrees for one hour. Serve warm.

Makes 6 to 8 servings.

EASY-PEASY BERRY COBBLER

JESSICA ZELKOVICH
GREENFIELD, IN

Tastes like summer...couldn't be simpler to make!

16-oz. pkg. frozen mixed berries
1/2 c. sugar
cinnamon to taste
12-oz. tube refrigerated biscuits

Pour frozen berries into a slow cooker and stir in sugar. Arrange biscuits on top; sprinkle with cinnamon to taste. Cover and cook on high setting for 3 hours. Serve warm.

Makes 8 to 12 servings.

EASY FRIED APPLE PIES

CAROLYN DECKARD
BEDFORD, IN

We have been fixing these fried pies for years while camping. I like to use different fillings each time to give everyone a favorite. To make this easier, I have been buying pie crust already rolled out, which saves a lot of time.

Prepare pie crust mix according to package directions. On a lightly floured surface, roll dough out 1/8 inch thick; cut into 6-inch circles, using a saucer for pattern. Re-roll remaining dough; cut into more circles and set aside. In a bowl, combine pie filling and cinnamon; place 1/4 cup of mixture on one-half of each circle. Top with one tablespoon cheese. Fold unfilled half over; press to seal with your fingers or a fork. In a heavy skillet, heat 1/4 inch oil to 375 degrees over medium-high heat. Add several pies at a time and cook until golden, about 3 to 4 minutes on each side. Remove carefully to paper towels; sprinkle with powdered sugar.

11-oz. pkg. pie crust mix
21-oz. can apple pie filling
1 t. cinnamon
1/2 c. shredded Cheddar cheese, divided
oil for frying
Garnish: powdered sugar

Makes 7 to 8 servings.

BUTTERSCOTCH SAUCE

SANDY ANN WARD
ANDERSON, IN

A favorite that Grandma used to make...scrumptious over ice cream and bread pudding.

Melt butter in a heavy saucepan over medium heat. Add brown sugar, cream and salt; stir with a spatula until well mixed. Bring to a boil. Boil for 4 to 5 minutes, scraping down sides of pan occasionally, until thickened and light in color. Remove from heat; stir in vanilla. Cover and refrigerate.

1/4 c. butter
1/8 t. salt
1 c. brown sugar, packed
1 t. vanilla extract
1/4 c. whipping cream

Makes about one cup.

GRANDMA ROSE'S CARROT CAKE

MARGE SCHICK
PORTAGE, IN

My grandmother came here in 1912 from Austria. My sisters can remember her making strudel with paper-thin dough and apple filling. While I don't remember that, I do remember her carrot cake. It was the best ever...none today even compare!

2 c. sugar
1/4 c. oil
4 eggs
1 t. vanilla extract
3 c. all-purpose flour
1 t. salt
4 t. baking powder
1 t. baking soda
2 t. cinnamon
2 c. carrots, peeled and grated
1 c. chopped walnuts

Beat sugar and oil together. Add eggs, one at a time, beating well after each addition. Stir in vanilla; set aside. Sift together dry ingredients until well blended; add to sugar mixture. Fold in carrots and nuts. Pour into a lightly greased and floured tube cake pan. Bake at 350 degrees for one hour, or until a toothpick inserted near the center comes out clean. Set aside to cool; turn cake out of pan. Spread Cream Cheese Frosting over cake.

Cream Cheese Frosting:
Beat cream cheese until smooth; add milk, vanilla and salt. Gradually beat in powdered sugar until smooth.

Serves 12.

CREAM CHEESE FROSTING

8-oz. pkg. cream cheese, softened
1 t. milk
1 t. vanilla extract
1/8 t. salt
16-oz. pkg. powdered sugar

HASTY PEACH COBBLER

CYNTHIA GREEN
WORTHINGTON, IN

This recipe is a lifesaver when you have last-minute dinner guests. Mix it up quick, pop it in the oven and by the time you've finished dinner, a scrumptious warm dessert is ready. Try it with other flavors of pie filling too.

In a bowl, mix together flour, sugar and baking powder. Add milk and stir to mix well. Dot a 9"x9" baking pan with butter; pour batter into pan. Spoon peaches over batter. Bake at 375 degrees for 30 minutes, until golden. Serve warm, topped with a scoop of ice cream.

Makes 6 servings.

1/2 c. all-purpose flour
1/2 c. sugar
1 t. baking powder
1/2 c. milk
2 T. butter, diced
21-oz. can peach pie filling
Garnish: vanilla ice cream

RHUBARB UPSIDE-DOWN CAKE

DONNA TENNANT
JASPER, IN

My grandmother used to grow rhubarb, and as a child I used to wonder why anyone would want to eat such a thing. Of course being a child and breaking off a piece and chewing on it would have given anyone that thought! But try it in this cake, and I promise you will flip for rhubarb!

Combine rhubarb, sugar and gelatin mix. Pour into a lightly greased 13"x9" baking pan. Sprinkle with marshmallows; set aside. Prepare cake batter according to package directions; pour over marshmallows. Bake at 350 degrees for 45 minutes. Let cool, then invert onto a cake plate to serve.

Serves 12.

3 c. rhubarb, diced
1-1/2 c. sugar
6-oz. pkg. strawberry gelatin mix
2 c. mini marshmallows
18-1/2 oz. pkg. yellow or white cake mix

MOM'S BLACKBERRY CAKE

RACHEL PENCE
HOPE, IN

*My mom makes this yummy cake each year for my birthday. This can
also be baked in a 13"x9" baking pan...simply bake for 40 minutes.*

18-1/2 oz. pkg. white
  cake mix with pudding

3-oz. pkg. red raspberry
  gelatin mix

1 c. oil

1/2 c. milk

4 eggs

1 c. blackberries

1 c. sweetened flaked
  coconut

1 c. chopped pecans

FROSTING

1/2 c. butter, softened

16-oz. pkg. powdered
  sugar

4 to 5 T. milk

1/2 c. blackberries,
  crushed

1/2 c. sweetened flaked
  coconut

1/2 c. chopped pecans

Combine dry cake and pudding mixes with oil and
milk; mix well. Add eggs, one at a time, beating well
after each addition. Fold in blackberries, coconut
and pecans. Pour into 3 greased 9" round cake
pans. Bake at 350 degrees for 25 to 30 minutes.
Cool for 10 minutes before removing to wire racks to
cool completely. Spread tops of layers with frosting
and assemble cake. Spread remaining frosting over
sides.

Frosting:
Beat together butter and powdered sugar. Add milk
and berries; beat for 2 minutes. Stir in coconut and
pecans.

Serves 10 to 12.

SUPER-EASY PUDDIN' CAKE

CRIS GOODE
MOORESVILLE, IN

My husband's favorite cake...it's always a hit at get-togethers! The fresh berries make it look special, but it is really simple to make. You can mix & match lots of flavor combinations, like butter pecan cake with butterscotch pudding and topped with pecans, yum! You can even lighten it up a bit with fat-free and sugar-free pudding.

Prepare cake mix according to package directions. Bake in 2 greased 9" round cake pans; cool. Prepare pudding mixes according to package directions. Place one cake layer on a cake platter; top with half the pudding. Place the other layer on top; cover with remaining pudding. Sprinkle berries on top of cake and serve.

18-1/4 oz. pkg. devil's food cake mix

2 3.4-oz. pkgs. instant chocolate pudding mix

2 c. raspberries

Makes 8 servings.

HAYS COOKIES

SHERILYN RANK
WARSAW, IN

My mom first sampled these brown sugar cookie bars at a church carry-in dinner. She asked for the recipe and when she received it later, there was no name given for the cookies. Because Mrs. Hays was the lady who gave her the recipe, Mom dubbed these "Hays Cookies" and we've known them that way ever since!

In a large bowl, mix together flour, butter, salt and 1/2 cup brown sugar. Press mixture into the bottom of a lightly greased 9"x9" baking pan; set aside. In a small bowl, mix together eggs, sugar and remaining brown sugar. Spoon over flour mixture in pan; sprinkle with nuts. Bake at 350 degrees for 30 minutes. Remove from oven; let stand for 10 minutes. Sprinkle with powdered sugar; cut into bars while still warm.

1-1/2 c. all-purpose flour

1/2 c. butter

1/2 t. salt

1 c. brown sugar, packed and divided

2 eggs, beaten

1/2 c. sugar

1/4 c. chopped pecans or walnuts

Garnish: 1 T. powdered sugar

Makes about 2 dozen.

CHOCOLATE-BUTTERSCOTCH PIE

KATHY GRASHOFF
FORT WAYNE, IN

This classic is a favorite from the 1930s.

3/4 c. brown sugar, packed
1/3 c. all-purpose flour
1/2 t. salt
2-1/2 c. milk
6 T. chocolate syrup
2 egg yolks, beaten
2 T. butter
1/2 t. vanilla extract
9-inch pie crust, baked
Garnish: whipped topping

Thoroughly combine brown sugar, flour and salt; stir in milk, chocolate syrup and egg yolks. Pour into a saucepan over medium heat and cook until thickened; stir constantly. Remove from heat; blend in butter and vanilla. Pour into pie crust; cool to room temperature. Refrigerate until firm; serve with a dollop of whipped topping.

Makes 8 servings.

PEANUT BUTTER POPCORN

MARGARET HOSTETLER
LAGRANGE, IN

This is a special treat that our three sons and their friends have enjoyed for years. Our sons are grown, but when they come home they have asked for peanut butter popcorn. I like to take this treat to parties whenever a snack is in order. Yum!

4 to 6 qts. popped popcorn
1 c. sugar
1 c. light corn syrup
1 c. creamy or crunchy peanut butter
Optional: 1 t. vanilla extract

Place popped corn in a large roasting pan; set aside. In a saucepan over medium heat, bring sugar and corn syrup to a rolling boil. Remove from heat; stir in peanut butter and vanilla, if using. Pour over popped corn and stir to coat. Cool; store in an airtight container.

Serves 10 to 12.

EASY PISTACHIO CAKE

SHARON DENNISON
FLOYDS KNOBS, IN

My mom has been making this great-tasting cake for years. It's so easy to bake & take to parties too, right in its pan.

In a large bowl, blend together dry cake mix, milk, water, oil and eggs until smooth. Add dry pudding mix; stir well. Mix in nuts, if using. Pour batter into a lightly greased 13"x9" baking pan. Bake at 325 degrees for 45 minutes. Check for doneness with a toothpick; bake an additional 5 to 10 minutes, if needed. Cool completely; spread Cream Cheese Icing over cooled cake.

Cream Cheese Icing:

In a large bowl, blend cream cheese, butter, vanilla and powdered sugar. Add enough milk for a spreadable consistency; stir in food coloring and nuts.

Serves 12 to 15.

18-1/2 oz. pkg. yellow or white cake mix
1/2 c. milk
1/2 c. water
1/2 c. oil
5 eggs, beaten
2 3.4-oz. pkgs. instant pistachio pudding mix
Optional: 1/2 c. chopped nuts

CREAM CHEESE ICING

8-oz. pkg. cream cheese, softened
1/4 c. butter, softened
1 t. vanilla extract
16-oz. pkg. powdered sugar
3 to 4 T. milk
1 to 2 drops green food coloring
3/4 c. chopped nuts

PUMPKIN SQUARES

NIKKI OLSON
MUNSTER, IN

A favorite during fall, but they're unbeatable any time of year.

4 eggs, beaten
1-2/3 c. sugar
1 c. oil
2 c. all-purpose flour
1-1/2 t. cinnamon
2 t. baking powder
2 t. baking soda
15-oz. can pumpkin
1/2 t. salt
Garnish: colored
sprinkles

Mix all ingredients except for garnish, for 2 to 3 minutes or until thoroughly blended; pour into a greased 15"x10" baking pan. Bake at 250 degrees for 50 to 60 minutes; cool. Frost with Cream Cheese Frosting; decorate with sprinkles.

Cream Cheese Frosting:
Combine all ingredients and beat until smooth and creamy.

Makes 2-1/2 dozen servings.

CREAM CHEESE FROSTING

1/2 c. margarine,
softened
2 c. powdered sugar
8-oz. pkg. cream cheese,
softened
1-1/2 t. vanilla extract

JUST FOR FUN

The North Pole actually doesn't get any letters for Santa Claus, believe it or not. Indiana does. Every year, the aptly named town Santa Claus, Indiana actually receives those letters in the thousands. Even better, each and every one of those letters do get a reply!

CRUNCHY DESSERT

LUCINDA LEWIS
BROWNSTOWN, IN

With its butter-pecan flavor and crisp cereal crunch, everyone will be asking for seconds.

Melt margarine and brown sugar together in a 10" skillet; add cereal, coconut and pecans. Toast until lightly brown and crisp; stir constantly. Spread half the mixture in an 11"x9" baking pan; set aside. Remove ice cream from carton; slice into 1/2-inch sections. Arrange slices over toasted cereal mixture; seal edges of ice cream together with a spatula. Sprinkle with remaining toasted cereal mixture; cover and freeze until ready to serve. Cut into squares with a knife warmed by running under hot water.

Makes 20 servings.

1/2 c. margarine
1 c. brown sugar, packed
2-1/2 c. bite-size crispy rice cereal squares, crushed
3-1/2 c. flaked coconut
1/2 c. chopped pecans
1/2 gal. vanilla ice cream

CRANBERRY-WALNUT COBBLER

KATHY GRASHOFF
FORT WAYNE, IN

Crisp fall days make me eager to begin baking again. Nothing says fall like cranberries and walnuts!

In an ungreased 9" pie plate, combine cranberries, walnuts and 1/2 cup sugar. Toss until coated; set aside. In a bowl, whisk together eggs, melted butter, remaining sugar and extract until blended. Fold in our and salt until combined. Pour batter over cranberry mixture. Bake at 350 degrees for 40 minutes, or until bubbly and crust is golden. Transfer to a wire rack to cool.

Serves 8.

2-1/2 c. fresh or frozen cranberries
3/4 c. chopped walnuts
1/2 c. plus 3/4 c. sugar, divided
2 eggs, beaten
3/4 c. butter, melted and slightly cooled
1/4 t. almond extract
1 c. all-purpose flour
1/8 t. salt

INDEX

INDEX continued

U.S. to METRIC RECIPE EQUIVALENTS

Volume Measurements

¼ teaspoon..................... 1 mL
½ teaspoon..................... 2 mL
1 teaspoon .... 5 mL
1 tablespoon = 3 teaspoons...... 15 mL
2 tablespoons = 1 fluid ounce .... 30 mL
¼ cup......................... 60 mL
⅓ cup......................... 75 mL
½ cup= 4 fluid ounces .... 125 mL
1 cup= 8 fluid ounces........... 250 mL
2 cups = 1 pint = 16 fluid ounces 500 mL
4 cups = 1 quart .... 1 L

Weights

1 ounce .... 30 g
4 ounces .... 120 g
8 ounces .... 225 g
16 ounces = 1 pound........... 450 g

Baking Pan Sizes

Square
8x8x2 inches .... 2 L = 20x20x5 cm
9x9x2 inches ...... 2.5 L = 23x23x5 cm

Rectangular
13x9x2 inches ..... 3.5 L = 33x23x5 cm

Loaf
9x5x3 inches .... 2 L = 23x13x7 cm

Round
8x1½ inches .... 1.2 L = 20x4 cm
9x1½ inches .... 1.5 L = 23x4 cm

Recipe Abbreviations

t. = teaspoon......... ltr. = liter
T. = tablespoon........ oz. = ounce
c. = cup............... lb. = pound
pt. = pint.............. doz. = dozen
qt. = quart............. pkg. = package
gal. = gallon........... env. = envelope

Oven Temperatures

300° F...............150° C
325° F...............160° C
350° F...............180° C
375° F...............190° C
400° F...............200° C
450° F...............230° C

Kitchen Measurements

A pinch = ⅛ tablespoon
1 fluid ounce = 2 tablespoons
3 teaspoons = 1 tablespoon
4 fluid ounces = ½ cup
2 tablespoons = ⅛ cup
8 fluid ounces = 1 cup
4 tablespoons = ¼ cup
16 fluid ounces = 1 pint
8 tablespoons = ½ cup
32 fluid ounces = 1 quart
16 tablespoons = 1 cup
16 ounces net weight = 1 pound
2 cups = 1 pint
4 cups = 1 quart
4 quarts = 1 gallon

Send us your favorite recipe

and the memory that makes it special for you!*

If we select your recipe for a brand-new **Gooseberry Patch** cookbook, your name will appear right along with it...and you'll receive a FREE copy of the book!

Submit your recipe on our website at

www.gooseberrypatch.com/sharearecipe

*Please include the number of servings and all other necessary information.

Have a taste for more?

Visit www.gooseberrypatch.com to join our Circle of Friends!

• Free recipes, tips and ideas plus a complete cookbook index
• Get mouthwatering recipes and special email offers delivered to your inbox.

You'll also love these cookbooks from **Gooseberry Patch**!

Our Best 5-Ingredient Fresh Family Recipes
A Year of Holidays
Autumn in a Jiffy
Christmas Comfort Foods
Classic Church Potlucks
Our Best Fast, Easy & Delicious Recipes
Grandma's Favorites
Made from Scratch
Mom's Best Sunday Suppers
Our Best Recipes for Cast-Iron Cooking

www.gooseberrypatch.com